Suffer

Books by Mother Teresa
available as Fount Paperbacks

Blessed Are You
Daily Prayer with Mother Teresa
Daily Readings with Mother Teresa
A Gift for God
Mother Teresa: Contemplative at
the Heart of the World
Heart of Joy
Living the Word
Love of Christ
One Heart Full of Love

Books about Mother Teresa

Mother Teresa – Her People and Her Work
by Desmond Doig
Something Beautiful for God
by Malcolm Muggeridge

Suffering into Joy

What Mother Teresa Teaches about True Joy

Prepared and edited by
Eileen Egan and Kathleen Egan, OSB

Fount
An Imprint of HarperCollins*Publishers*

Found Paperbacks is an Imprint of
HarperCollins*Religious*
Part of HarperCollins*Publishers*
77–85 Fulham Palace Road, London W6 8JB

First published in the United States of America in
1994 by Servant Publications of Ann Arbor, Michigan

This edition first published in Great Britain
in 1995 by Fount Paperbacks

1   3   5   7   9   10   8   6   4   2

A catalogue record for this book is
available from the British Library

ISBN 0 00 627928-7

Typeset by Harper Phototypesetters Limited
Northampton, England
Printed and bound in Great Britain by
HarperCollinsManufacturing Glasgow

This book is dedicated to
Mabel Egan Gil,
to her deacon husband, Joseph Gil,
and to their family

Contents

❦

Do not be surprised, beloved, that a trial by fire is occurring in your midst. It is a test for you, but it should not catch you off guard. Rejoice instead, in the measure that you share Christ's sufferings. When his glory is revealed, you will rejoice exultantly.

1 Peter 4:12–13

1
The Face of Suffering in Today's World

❦

For I was hungry and you gave me food, I was thirsty and you gave me drink. I was a stranger and you welcomed me, naked and you clothed me. I was ill and you comforted me, in prison and you came to visit me.' Then the just will ask him: 'Lord, when did we see you hungry and feed you or see you thirsty and give you drink? . . .' The King will answer them, 'I assure you, as often as you did it for one of my least brothers, you did it for me.
   Matthew 25:35–40

We picked our way among the masses of brown bodies packed into the waiting room of the cavernous Sealdah Railway Station: women in discoloured saris, men with chests like birdcages and cloth *dhotis* wrapped around their loins, children half or wholly naked. It was Calcutta in 1955, and I* had just met a small vigorous woman in her mid-forties who had been receiving American goods through my agency, Catholic Relief Services. My stay could not be long because I was booked to fly from Calcutta to Saigon (now Ho Chi Minh City).

This unknown woman, wearing a sari with its wrap-around headpiece, introduced some young Indian women

---

*The use of the word 'I' throughout the text refers to Eileen Egan, who travelled and served with Mother Teresa for over thirty years.

dressed in similar garb who were ladling out a sort of gruel from steaming vats. Then she spoke directly to me: 'They like the rice,' said Mother Teresa. I knew that we had supplied the rice, parboiled wheat and soy that was now being poured into all kinds of receptacles, including brass pots. 'There must be over a thousand people here in Sealdah – and another 10,000 in the area,' she added, referring to the latest refugees from across the border of nearby Pakistan. Over a million destitute refugees had already cascaded into Calcutta since the subcontinent had been partitioned into India and Pakistan in 1947.

Through the experience with Catholic Relief Services, the overseas aid arm of the American Catholic community, I had become intimately acquainted with the face of human suffering and massive human pain. I had seen Europeans digging out of huge heaps of war ruins, and mourning those who had perished in them. I had worked in a camp for Polish survivors of deportation into Siberia. I knew the camps of the 'displaced persons'. Eastern Europeans dragooned into forced labour to serve the dreadful war machine. I had talked with a special group of displaced persons, the survivors of the Holocaust, and I had listened to their stories of unspeakable suffering. Now, in Asia, the face of suffering was intrusively and excruciatingly evident.

'After Sealdah, we will go to Shishu Bhavan, and then Nirmal Hriday,' said Mother Teresa. Shishu Bhavan was the Children's Home, whose children were the city's throwaways. Mother Teresa explained that some children had been found in rubbish heaps; some had been brought in when their mothers had died. 'We do our best to nurse them back to life,' Mother Teresa explained, cradling a baby with a wizened little face and tiny limbs. 'There is life in him,' she added. 'The life of Jesus is in him.'

Nirmal Hriday means 'Pure or Immaculate Heart'. Mother Teresa told me that Nirmal Hriday, also referred to as 'Kalighat', had been opened in 1952, when the City Fathers of Calcutta gave her the use of the former pilgrims' hostel. Kalighat took its name from the nearby shrine to Kali, and from *ghat*, which refers to the broad steps leading to a nearby river bank where the dead were carried for cremation. I entered it fearfully. This Home of the Dying in the pilgrims' hall near the Kali temple was often the final refuge for those found breathing their last on the streets and in the gutters of the anguished city.

I watched Mother Teresa as she sat on the parapet next to the low pallets of men, patting their heads or stroking their stick-like arms, murmuring to each one. Sometimes only the eyes seemed alive in men whose skin was drawn so tightly that the skull seemed struggling to burst through. Some were even smiling, as though amazed to be alive. It was the same in the women's hall. Seeing me, they held out their wasted hands, searching for human consolation. I turned away in fear and shame. I wondered how she could face, day after day, caring for those who were brought in covered with the filth and spittle of the gutter.

Mother Teresa explained that her work and the work of the Sisters called for them to see Jesus in everyone, including the men and women dying in the gutter. She said:

They are Jesus. Everyone is Jesus in a distressing disguise.

This overpowering concept is what I carried away from my first of many visits to Calcutta and my first of many encounters and travels with Mother Teresa.

From Calcutta With Love

❧

In the earlier days of Mother Teresa's ministry there were those who had wondered about her calling to the streets of Calcutta, as they watched her don the garb of the poorest woman, living out her 'call within a call'.

> In the choice of work, there was neither planning nor preconceived ideas. We started our work as the suffering of the people called us. God showed us what to do.

Soon after the founding of the Society in 1950, young women began to fill the novitiate training centre at the Mother House in Calcutta. Teams of five or six were soon on their way all over India. Additional teams of Sisters founded slum schools, conducted Mother and Child clinics, and went by ambulance to clusters of leper patients in and around Calcutta. Eventually, sixty centres brought loving care to the mothers and children of every slum in Calcutta.

By 1965, the Missionaries of Charity were recognized as an international Society by the Church. Now they were a group that could go wherever Church authorities and local officials invited them. The only provision, according to the rule of the Society, was that the work should be 'right on the ground', and serve the 'poorest of the poor'. Soon, the Missionaries of Charity were in demand around the world. Mother Teresa responded by sending teams of Sisters to Harlem and the South Bronx in New York City; to poor areas of Rome; to cities in Africa, the Caribbean and Latin America; and to the aboriginal peoples of Australia.

The work of Mother Teresa and the Missionaries of Charity first became known to the public through the book *Something Beautiful for God* by Malcolm Muggeridge. It was published in 1971 and was translated into many languages. Later, a documentary film *Mother Teresa*, made by Ann and Jeanette Petrie, brought the drama of the works of mercy to countless people through television showings and videotapes.

Young women, fired by the blazing witness of the Missionaries of Charity, poured into the training centres that were set up in various parts of the world. In addition to the first novitiate in Calcutta, later novitiates were opened in the Philippines, in Europe, in Africa, and in the United States. As the work developed, over 500 small teams of Sisters brought works of mercy into some 105 countries and areas of the world.

In 1986 Pope John Paul II came to the Home for Dying in Calcutta, to comfort those whom Mother Teresa called 'her treasures'. She called that day 'the happiest day of my life'. The visit of the Holy Father to her most dramatic work of love validated her whole life's work of serving Jesus in 'his most distressing disguise'.

From 1988 onward, Mother Teresa took Sisters to Poland, Eastern Europe, and the former Soviet Union. In 1990 they began to work in Siberia, and in 1991 in Albania.

On 2 June 1993 Mother Teresa was made a Freeman of the city of Dublin. She was the first nun to receive the honour. Spiritual leaders of many denominations joined with Irish government officials for the ceremony. On that day, this capital city put aside its other business in order to honour the woman who had come there sixty-five years before to begin her life as a religious sister in the Mother House of the Sisters of Loreto. From Dublin she had gone out to form a new religious family that spanned the globe.

The Mystery of Suffering

🍂

If one were to ask what is the most enduring challenge of people of faith, many would answer in one word: suffering. Sometimes suffering, especially the suffering of the innocent and the just, is seen as an evil, presenting an unfathomable mystery. In the secret places of the heart, it is sometimes harder to bear the knowledge that God allows his own children to suffer such misery – without his direct intervention – than to endure physical pain. Where is God while his children destroy each other? Where is the justice of God when children suffer and die in the prime of life? Does God cause suffering?

Pope John Paul II, in his February 1984 Apostolic Letter, *The Christian Meaning of Human Suffering*, states: 'At one and the same time Christ has taught man to do good by his suffering and to do good to those who suffer. In this double aspect, he has completely revealed the meaning of suffering.' In a special way, Mother Teresa illustrates the living out of this double aspect. A symbol of hope in the midst of almost overpowering darkness and poverty, Mother Teresa teaches that suffering can be turned to good to produce true joy in the heart of a believer.

When Mother Teresa visited former President Ronald Reagan at the White House shortly after an assassin's bullet nearly ended his life, she pointed out to the President the good that could come even out of his brush with death:

You have suffered the passion of the cross. There is a purpose in this. Because of your suffering and pain, you will now understand the suffering and pain of the world.

With these words Mother Teresa would encourage anyone, even the poorest among us, struck down by an unexpected attack or by an illness. Whereas suffering can embitter a person, hardening the heart against those who have inflicted the suffering, Mother Teresa reminds us that suffering can also serve to enlarge the heart of the afflicted one, enabling him or her to experience compassion for the sufferings of others.

Compassion, Mother Teresa's life tells us, always finds its fullest expression in deeds, in the works of mercy performed sacrificially. Indeed, her life is a profound witness to the manner in which suffering ultimately works for the good of the human family. For Mother Teresa, compassion is essential to any work done in the name of Jesus. Compassion opens the heart of persons to the pain of others and moves them to works of mercy. As she pointed out in the Home for the Dying, however, her motivation is deeper than natural compassion.

Again, in the words of Pope John Paul II: 'The world of human suffering unceasingly calls for, so to speak, another world, the world of human love, and in a certain sense man owes to human suffering that unselfish love which stirs in his heart and actions' (*The Christian Meaning of Human Suffering*). Mother Teresa and the Missionaries of Charity, face to face with hopelessness, misery and death, give breathtaking witness to the world of human love, and amazingly, they give it with joy. To her Sisters Mother Teresa wrote:

> In the slums we are the light of God's kindness to the poor. To the children, to all who suffer and are lonely, give always a happy smile. Give them not only your care but also your heart.

How is it possible to emerge from such human squalor with

such a message of joy? That is Mother Teresa's gift. To her, the pain and agony she relieves are that of the Saviour himself. Therefore each person she serves has an inviolable dignity and sacredness.

We read in the New Testament accounts of Jesus' sufferings. How many of us would long to have been present when Jesus was ill-treated and spat upon? Mother Teresa reminds us that we are not born too late to show our love to Jesus, to console him, to clothe him, to slake his thirst, to feed him in his hunger. This conviction, that meeting others' needs shows mercy to Jesus in his 'distressing disguise', can only be achieved by the inspiration of the Holy Spirit, which is nourished by prayer. By joining their poverty and privation with the sufferings of Jesus, Mother Teresa and the Sisters share in the joy of the redemption, the great drama of the saving of the world. Not only is their suffering turned into joy, but they bring joy into the lives of others.

To the Missionaries of Charity and to all who serve others, Mother Teresa says:

> Keep giving Jesus to your people not by words, but by your example, by your being in love with Jesus, by radiating his holiness and spreading his fragrance of love everywhere you go. Just keep the *joy* of Jesus as your strength. Be happy and at peace. Accept whatever he gives – and give whatever he takes with a big smile. You belong to him.

2
Doing the Work of Jesus:
The Missionaries of Charity

❦

> When a woman is in labour she is sad that her time has
> come. When she has borne her child, she no longer
> remembers her pain for joy that a man has been born into
> the world. In the same way, you are sad for a time, but I
> shall see you again; then your hearts will rejoice with a
> joy no one can take from you.
>   *John 16:21-2*

Mother Teresa recognizes the importance of the contribution of social workers to the welfare of society. Yet she
makes an important distinction between the role of the
Missionaries of Charity and that of other people attending
to the physical needs of the poor:

> Jesus wanted to help by sharing our life, our loneliness,
> our agony, our death. Only by being one with us has he
> redeemed us. We are allowed to do the same; all the
> desolation of the poor people, not only their material
> poverty, but their spiritual destitution, must be redeemed,
> and we must share it, for only by being one with them can
> we redeem them, that is, by bringing God into their lives
> and bringing them to God.

The Sisters are asked to follow joyfully a path that contra-
dicts the values of a culture that honours, even glorifies,

ease and pleasure. They are to accept willingly whatever difficulty or suffering that may come to them from their closeness to the poor. Only the conviction that Jesus is in every poor or afflicted person could make their way of life possible, as Mother Teresa asserts:

> Without our suffering, our work would be just social work – it would not be the work of Jesus Christ, not part of the redemption.

When the young women in blue-bordered white saris came to New York City in 1981 they were seen as social workers. Mother Teresa, on a morning television programme, was described simply as a 'humanitarian'; her motivation was not relevant to their interview. By then, the Missionaries of Charity had become an international community. The faces framed by the wrap-around headcovering were all different, representing just about every nation under heaven – yet all with the same spirit.

Public wonderment still greets the Sisters today. With their choice of serving 'the poorest of the poor' comes poverty, separation from all the goods of consumerism. With their choice comes the renunciation of marriage and children. With their choice comes a life of obedience and a rigid schedule that starts with rising at five o' clock in the morning.

When I asked a young Englishwoman working in the South Bronx how she had come to join Mother Teresa's Society, she replied, 'I had what a lot of young women would want. I had a fine job as a literary agent – interesting work, meeting a variety of people. I had my own flat, a car, yet my life lacked meaning. The deeper meaning I found when I came to know the Missionaries of Charity.' By alleviating human need in the name of the Lord, she had found joy and peace of mind, and a life of meaning.

The Fourth Vow

❧

As with other religious orders, the Missionaries of Charity make three promises or vows: vows of poverty, chastity and obedience. In addition, the Missionaries of Charity take a special fourth vow, that of 'whole-hearted and free service to the poorest of the poor'. They will never graduate from their place on the lowest rung with God's children. If the poor they serve rise out of poverty, the Sisters move down, finding poorer people to serve – those who have fallen through the cracks of whatever social support system exists. The Sisters seek out those who are shunned and abandoned, the 'throw-away people' of the societies in which they live and minister.

All Missionaries of Charity, already trained in the spirit of the work, carry with them a copy of their rule. Those of us who have seen young Sisters in Calcutta's Home for the Dying, cleaning the spittle and filth from men and women from the gutter, know how their rule is put into practice. In other parts of the world, the Sisters choose to live near the garbage dumps of great cities like Mexico City or Cairo, so as to serve the garbage pickers. Their motivation could only come from seeing service to these impoverished men, women and children as a response to the call of Christ.

Mother Teresa assigns the highest dignity to those who are deprived and feel themselves the least members of society. She writes in the Constitution of the Missionaries of Charity:

> We need to be pure of heart to see Jesus in the person of
> the poor. Therefore, the more repugnant the work, or the
> more disfigured or deformed the image of God in the
> person, the greater will be our faith and devotion in seeing

the face of Jesus, and lovingly minister to him in the distressing disguise.

The Constitution further guides the Sisters with words that bind them equally to the poorest of the poor and to each other:

> Our response to the call of Christ is our fourth vow by which we bind ourselves to give whole-hearted and free service to the poorest of the poor according to obedience and so to ceaselessly quench the thirst of Jesus.

Three words of this vow have special significance to the Sisters: *whole-hearted, free* and *service*.

Whole-hearted means:

- with hearts burning with zeal and love for souls
- with single-minded devotion, wholly rooted in our deep union with God in prayer and fraternal love
- we give them not only our hands to serve, but our hearts also, to love with kindness and humility
- entirely at the disposal of the poor
- hard labour without counting the cost.

Free means:

- joyfully and with eagerness
- fearlessly and openly
- freely giving what we have freely received
- without accepting any return in cash or kind
- without seeking any reward or gratitude.

Service means:

- an unceasing and whole-hearted labour in making ourselves available to Jesus so that he may live, in and through us, his life of infinitely tender, compassionate and merciful love for the spiritually and materially poorest of the poor

- immediate and effective service to the poorest of the poor, as long as they have no one to help them, by:
  - feeding the hungry; not only with food, but also with the Word of God
  - giving drink to the thirsty; not only for water, but for knowledge, peace, truth, justice and love
  - clothing the naked; not only with clothes, but also with human dignity
  - giving shelter to the homeless; not only a shelter made of bricks, but a heart that understands, that covers, that loves
  - nursing the sick and dying; not only of the body but also of mind and spirit.

The Brothers of Charity

❧

This same spirit of service is seen in the Missionary Brothers of Charity, founded in 1963, thirteen years after Mother Teresa's founding of the Missionaries of Charity. The Brothers followed the Sisters in taking the fourth vow of 'whole-hearted and free service to the poorest of the poor', and in going to society's 'throw-aways'. One of their works was to open a shelter for Calcutta's street boys.

The head of the Missionary Brothers of Charity is called the 'General Servant'. This first General Servant, Brother Andrew, who was released by the Society of Jesus for this task, describes the service of the Brothers: 'The joys of work with the suffering poor are many and deep. There is the joy of seeing people relieved of at least a little of their suffering, of the sick cured, of families finding employment for a bread-winner, of children of the streets finding a home . . . overcoming difficulties.'

Brother Andrew goes on to tell of a homeless five-year-old boy who was found on a railway station platform beside his dead mother and dying father. The boy and his father were taken to the shelter, where the man died a few days later. Instead of giving up after the deaths of his parents, recalls Brother Andrew, the boy, who had only one leg, seemed to come to life and began to laugh and play with his new little brothers at the shelter, who had been similarly touched with love.

'There is great joy in seeing a little one-legged boy from the railway station playing happily in the room with me,' smiles Brother Andrew. 'Now he finds a home, food and a little love. Such sights and experiences are a great encouragement and happiness. I think that the faith and love of those from afar who share in the work is much greater, for they do not have the consolation of seeing the light in young eyes, or hearing the laughter and singing.'

The Love of a Parent

❧

I was wondering how I could explain to myself the tenderness of the Sisters in their lowly work as I watched a Sister console a dying mother with AIDS in 'The Gift of Love', the AIDS hospice in Washington, DC. I was reminded of passages in the Book of John where Jesus compares the suffering of his followers with childbirth. A mother forgets her suffering with which that child entered the world, and simply loves her baby. She doesn't tally up the loss of sleep, the constant feeding and washing, and the special care the child may need when sickness strikes. Love for her child motivates everything she does.

A mother's love becomes even more remarkable in the most difficult situations. Because she is the mother, her love supersedes natural affection for the attractive. She works even harder to tenderly serve the child who is afflicted with the grossest deformities, the child who may never have the full use of arms, legs or mental faculties. Her love is inextinguishable.

Mother Teresa tells the story of this kind of love, in this case a father's love for a child adopted from the Children's Home, the Shishu Bhavan, in Calcutta. Mother Teresa recalls:

> One of the abandoned children we had in our Shishu Bhavan I gave to a very high-class and rich family. After a few months I heard that the child had become very sick and completely disabled. So I went to that family and said, 'Give me back the child and I will give you a healthy child.' The father looked at me and said, 'Take my life first, then take the child.' He loved the child from his heart.
>
> In Calcutta, every night we send word to all the clinics, to all the police stations, to all the hospitals, 'Please do not destroy any children; we will take them all.' So our house is always full of children. There is a joke in Calcutta: 'Mother Teresa is always talking about family planning and abortion, but every day she has more and more children.'

On another occasion, Mother Teresa spoke of the tenderness she found in God the Father, depicted in Isaiah:

> I have called you by name; you are mine.
> When you pass through the water,
> I will be with you;
> in the rivers you shall not drown.
> When you walk through fire,

you shall not be burned;
the flames shall not consume you.
Isaiah 43:1–2

See, upon the palms of my hands I
have written your name.
Isaiah 49:16

When Mother Teresa visited Cuba, Premier Castro treated her and her companions with respect as they discussed the work of the Missionaries of Charity around the world. But when Mother Teresa offered to bring the Sisters to Cuba to serve the poor, Premier Castro declined her offer with thanks, explaining that, in Cuba, the Government provided for the people, giving them what they needed. Mother Teresa did not argue with the Head of State. She said simply, 'But the Government cannot give love.'

As it turned out, not long afterwards several teams of Sisters were in fact invited to come to the island nation. Cuba's shaky economy had depended for many years on financial support from the Soviet Union but this aid was discontinued when the Cold War ended. Arriving in Cuba, the Sisters found much suffering as a result of this massive political shift. They were able to open two houses to care, with the love of Jesus, for members of the poorest families who were terminally ill.

Simplicity of Faith

❧

Wherever they are, the Missionaries of Charity start the day's work with the same prayer from their community prayer book. From Novosibirsk to Papua New Guinea; from Bucharest to Hong Kong; from Madras to Bourke, Australia, they ask for strength in lifting up the burden of suffering. This they consider their privilege. This is their joy.

> Dear Lord, the Great Healer, I kneel before you, since every perfect gift must come from you. I pray, give skill to my hands, clear vision to my mind, kindness and meekness to my heart. Give me singleness of purpose, strength to lift up a part of the burden of my suffering fellow men, and a realization of the privilege that is mine. Take from my heart all guile and worldliness, that with the simple faith of a child, I may rely on you. Amen.

In reciting the prayer, each Sister reiterates her total dependence on God the Father. Besides praying for a pure and eager heart and strong arms, the Sisters rely entirely on God's provision for the material needs of the day. The Missionaries of Charity in each house use their faith as a kind of heavenly currency to provide for the expenses of serving the poor.

Mother Teresa herself invariably stresses this dependence. I think back to the steaming vats of food in the courtyard and the families who were kept alive by our gifts of regular food. I recall her spirited sharing:

> We have to pull out the wonderful things that are happening in the world. Now we feed more than 9,000 people in Shishu Bhavan every day.

One day, Mother Teresa beckoned us to stand in front of the world map with its little markers all over India, Asia, Australia, the Middle East, Africa, Latin America and North America. 'All those houses,' she said. 'Two hundred and fifty-seven, I think. A hundred and twenty in India.' Mother Teresa traced the outline of China until her finger found Beijing. 'That is where we must go.' Continuing to gaze at the map, she said:

Look what God is doing with nothing. People must believe
that it is all his, all his. We must allow God to use us,
without adding or subtracting anything.

Her earlier statement came back to me:

I am more convinced of the work being his than I am
convinced that I am really alive.

3
A Cheerful Heart:
Renouncing All for Christ

❧

As we have shared much in the suffering of Christ, so through Christ do we share abundantly in his consolation. If we are afflicted it is for your encouragement and salvation, and when we are consoled it is for your consolation, so that you may endure patiently the same suffering we endure. Our hope for you is firm because we know that just as you share in the sufferings, so you will share in the consolation.
2 Corinthians 1:5–7

In *Something Beautiful for God*, Malcolm Muggeridge remarked:

Spending a few days with you, I have been immensely struck by the joyfulness of these Sisters who do what an outsider might think to be almost impossibly difficult and painful tasks.

Mother Teresa explained: 'That's the spirit of our Society, that total surrender, loving trust and cheerfulness. We must be able to radiate the joy of Christ, express it in our actions. If our actions are just useful actions that give no joy to the people, our poor people would never be able to rise up to the call which we want them to hear, the call to come closer to God. We want to make them feel that they are loved. If we went to them with a sad face, we would only make them much more depressed.'

Return to the Home for the Dying

❦

In Calcutta, I myself saw how the Missionaries of Charity start the day with joy, coming as they do from Mass, from receiving the Communion of the Bread of Life and the Saving Cup.

This time when I went in the van to Kalighat, the Home for the Dying, I discovered I was no longer afraid; I had lost the trepidation I felt the first time I'd crossed the threshold. I was no longer a stranger here. In addition, I had taken the precautions my doctors had ordered, and my shameful memory of turning away from the dying on my earlier visit was lessened by my sense of personal contribution to the work in the Sisters' many outposts.

Catholic Relief Services had been making regular shipments of food and medicaments from Food for Peace stocks, and these had to be warehoused and marked for distribution to Mother Teresa's centres in Calcutta, in Krishnagar and other parts of Bengal, as well as Bihar and Orissa. We needed a fuller port staff and more administrative staff in Calcutta, and I had determined that finding these workers would be my special task. In time I had become acquainted with the port area where an incredible array of relief goods was unloaded. Before long the staff of Catholic Relief Services was increased in size, which in turn allowed the feeding programme and other relief programmes to expand. It was exciting to see the famished being fed and countless lives being saved.

Charubala was an older woman I came to know at the Home for the Dying. She was truly the least of all. She could not walk, but could sit up on her pallet to eat her meals. Her grey hair was cropped close to her head, a sign that she was a widow. She had been an object of pity and disdain in her village, relegated to a life of near-slavery by her widow-hood. This was despite the fact that her marriage, arranged for her when she was a small child, had never been consummated: the man to whom she had been promised had died before she was old enough to marry.

In Hindu society a woman's status and protection both come from her husband. Therefore, the death of her husband is the worst fate that can befall a woman. The ancient custom of *suttee*, by which a woman threw herself on her husband's funeral pyre to be consumed with him, indicated the hopelessness of the Hindu widow's plight. The practice of *suttee* had been done away with by British rule, but this did not address the cultural attitude behind the custom. For this reason, Charubala's story was not unique. Widows were still among the most impoverished of that society, with no one to look after them. When she had become disabled, Charubala had been cast out into the street. But she had been found and transported by the Sisters to the Home for the Dying.

We regularly went from pallet to pallet. There were greet-ings and chats in Hindi and Bengali, and in English for the few Anglo-Indians. I saw how Charubala's great brown eyes shone as Mother Teresa or a Sister came near her. When they put a caressing hand on Charubula's shorn head, she responded with intense joy. It was overpowering. Sometimes, she even burst into a Bengali song. I found myself included in her grateful response. Over and over again, I marvelled at the contented peace of these men and women from whom every-thing had been taken. I marvelled much more at the joy that was returned by them to their caretakers.

As time went on, I began to look forward to going to Kalighat. I knew many of the men and women, and they knew me. They appreciated my few words of Bengali, and even in their pain and weakness would hold out almost fleshless hands for me to hold and caress.

We took special care of those newly brought in from the street, that they would not over-eat after having hungered for so long. The effort was to make them feel loved and cared for. One time, I was able to help carry an aged and famished woman into the Home for the Dying. Her eyes were at first fearful, then tranquil as I fed her, spoonful by spoonful, her first meal. As I cradled her head to support her and prevent her from choking, I realized that the woman needed this gesture of tenderness almost as much as the food itself.

The Gift of Love

❦

'This is perfect joy – to share in the sufferings of the world as Christ did,' said St Francis of Assisi. The people who listened to St Francis in his day found it hard to consent to this response to Jesus. So does our world today, when the words come from the mouth of Mother Teresa. And yet many people took the *poverello*, the 'little poor man', at his word and chose to follow St Francis in the vowed life. Countless men and women then and now find that his word and his life resonate in the deepest recesses of their hearts. St Francis and Mother Teresa strike a universal chord that asserts a mysterious affinity between suffering and joy.

Mother Teresa prays:

Lord, help us to see, in your crucifixion and resurrection, an example of how to endure and seemingly to die, in the agony and conflict of daily life, so that we may live more fully and more creatively. . . . Enable us to go through [trials] patiently and bravely, trusting that you will support us; for it is only by dying with you that we can rise with you. Amen.

After returning from her visit to prisoners with AIDS in a jail near New York City, Mother Teresa commented that she had learned something from the people who suffer from AIDS. She had learned in a new way the need for greater compassion, the need for a renewed work of the tender love we all have inside, whether we are sick or healthy. She said:

God is giving us something so that we can show that tender love, that concern. This sickness has come to teach us something, to open our eyes to the need of the tender love that we all have and that has been forgotten, been pushed out. I remember when those people with AIDS were in jail and we had to sit in that jail, one said, 'I don't want to die here, I don't want to die in jail.' And then, thank God, we prayed and prayed to Our Lady, and then we called the governor and the mayor. A big miracle, I believe, happened. Within a few hours the men were released from prison.

We call our home in Washington, DC, 'The Gift of Love'. One of the AIDS patients had to leave the home to go to the hospital. When I visited him, he said to me, 'Mother Teresa, you are my friend. I want to talk to you alone.'

What did he say after twenty-five years of being away from God? 'When I get the terrible pain in my head, I share it with Jesus and suffer as he did when he was crowned with thorns. When I get the terrible pain in my back, I share it with him when he was scourged at the pillar, and when I get the pain in my hands and feet, I share it with him when he was nailed to the cross. I ask you to take me home. I want to die with you.'

I got permission and took him to our home, The Gift of

Love, and took him into the chapel. I never heard anyone
talk to Jesus like this man talked to him, so tenderly, so full
of love. Three days later he died.

The Joy of Renunciation

❧

Besides the young women who specifically choose to be
'part of the redemption' as vowed Missionaries of Charity,
there are people around the world of all faiths who respond
to Mother Teresa's way of life. This way of life is an enigma
to non-Christians and worldly Christians alike. Such teach-
ings point to the true source of joy. Mother Teresa's life
shows to us the surprising places where joy can be found.
As she writes in the Constitution:

> Renunciation is one of these places. Our life of penance
> will have that twofold quality of renunciation and joy, since
> it is deeply rooted in the mystery of the cross and
> resurrection.
>
> Joy is indeed the fruit of the Holy Spirit and a
> characteristic mark of the Kingdom of God, for God is joy.
> Christ wanted to share his joy with his apostles ' . . . that my
> joy may be in you, and that your joy may be full' (John 15:11
> RSV). Joy is prayer, the sign of our generosity, selflessness,
> and close and continual union with God. Joy is love – a
> joyful heart is the normal result of a heart burning with love.

She has said to her Sisters:

> Keep the joy of loving God, loving Jesus in your heart, and
> share that joy with all you meet.

More and more every day I realized the importance of
Mother Teresa's insistence that the Missionaries of Charity

renounce gloominess along with everything else of the world. She requires that the Sisters be persons of cheerful disposition in their work with people who lead deprived lives. 'A joyful Sister', she says, 'is like the sunshine of God's love.'

'Joy', affirms the guideline of the Society, 'is a net of love by which we catch souls. A Sister filled with joy preaches without preaching. Joy is a need and a power for us even physically, for it makes us always ready to go about doing good. "The joy of the Lord is your strength." (Nehemiah 8:10 RSV)'

When one of the Sisters, wearing a mournful expression on her face, was getting ready to visit the poor, Mother Teresa said, 'Don't go. Go back to bed. We cannot meet the poor with sad faces.'

Even in small things, Mother Teresa does not tolerate long faces. Sitting with a group of volunteers who were dispirited after working with the needy, she joked about a traveller whose car broke down at the edge of a lonely, barren region. The only refuge was a monastery and the only means of transportation the monks could offer the man was a donkey. The traveller insisted on continuing his journey, so the monks explained that to manage the animal the man must remember to say 'Amen, Amen' when he wanted it to stop, but 'Thank God, thank God' when he wanted it to go forward.

All went well until a precipice yawned before him, and the nervous man remembered just in time to shout 'Amen, Amen'. The donkey stopped at the very edge of the precipice. Then the man said fervently, 'Thank God' – and over he went!

No one laughed harder than Mother Teresa herself, who is known for saying 'Thank God' on any and every occasion.

Other times, she recounts humorous incidents from her

daily rounds. For example, she recalls trying to help a woman on a street in London. The woman, who was very drunk, turned to her saying, 'Mother Teresa, didn't Jesus turn the water into wine for us to enjoy it?'

As St Francis said to his many followers, recorded in Thomas Celano's *St Francis of Assisi*: 'For what else are servants of God, but minstrels, whose work it is to lift up people's hearts and move them to spiritual gladness?'

The Joy of Service

❦

While Mother Teresa daily sees intense suffering, she sees joy as the heart of the Good News. In the Constitution of the Missionaries of Charity she writes:

> In Bethlehem, 'Joy' said the angel; Christ wanted to share his joy with his Apostles – 'that my joy may be with you'. *Joy* was the password of the first Christians; St Paul often repeats, 'Rejoice in the Lord always; again I say to you, rejoice.' In return for the great grace of baptism, the priest tells the newly baptized, 'May you serve the Church joyfully.'

Mother Teresa teaches that true joy must come from God. Teaching Sisters, for example, can become easily discouraged to the point of becoming 'burned out', especially after serving year after year in deprived neighbourhoods. Some wonder if they will ever succeed in reaching those they are serving. For these people, Mother Teresa says simply:

> God has not called us to be successful. He has called us to be faithful.

When a group of American teachers visited the work in

Calcutta, they asked for some advice to take home to their families. 'Smile at your wives,' Mother Teresa told them. 'Smile at your husbands.'

This advice seemed surprising, coming from an unmarried person. One of them asked, 'Are you married?'

'Yes,' she answered. 'And I find it very hard sometimes to smile at Jesus. He can be very demanding.'

In a talk to the teaching Sisters of the diocese of Scranton, Pennsylvania, Mother Teresa reminded them of the password of the ancestors of all Christians living in the world, those early Christians who so often faced brutal persecution:

> We are all working together, to bring Christ to the university or high school or right down to the slums. We are doing it together. The work that you do is his gift to you. Today, talking about the poor is in fashion. Knowing, loving and serving the poor is quite another matter. The little St Thérèse said, 'In the heart of the Church, I will be love.' That is what we are, love in the heart of the Church. The password of the early Christians was joy. Serve the Lord with joy.

4
The Suffering of the Innocent

❦

> . . . but we do see Jesus crowned with glory and honour
> because he suffered death: Jesus, who was made for a little
> while lower than the angels, that through God's gracious
> will he might taste death for the sake of all men.
> *Hebrews 2:9*

At a Eucharistic Congress, timed with the celebration of the
United States' Bicentennial in 1976, Mother Teresa was the
centre of attention. In a stadium filled with 8,000 people she
was called upon to speak on the role of women in the
Church. People ran after her, tugged at her sari, begged for
advice, or simply asked for her prayers. Those days of the
Congress were among the most trying days of her life. But
nothing could stop Mother Teresa from responding to the
call of people who needed her – for encouragement, for
consolation, or merely for a smile.

One of those was a mother who brought her tiny baby to
Mother Teresa. The mother explained that her ten-week-old
daughter had Down's Syndrome. She knew that the child
would need complete care for the rest of her life. The infant
also needed a heart operation. The mother kept repeating,
through falling tears, 'I want my child to live. Pray, Mother
Teresa, that my Shannon will live.'

Mother Teresa put her hand gently on the little head,
noting the pallid face and limp hands. She spoke gently for

some time to the mother. I heard her say, 'God has given you this great gift of life. If God wants you to give the gift back to him, give it willingly, with love.'

Later, the mother wrote to Mother Teresa to tell her that Shannon had died when she was seven months old. Mother Teresa's words had given her courage throughout her grieving. There was no trace of bitterness in the mother as she faced the great mystery of the suffering and death of an innocent child.

The Bread of Life and Co-Redemption

❧

During the Eucharistic Congress her face was drawn with tiredness, yet Mother Teresa continued to respond to invitations to speak at a number of evening events. One of these was a Mass for young people. Large numbers of young people, prior to the youth meeting, had started a programme called SIGN, which stood for 'Service in God's Name'. In the spirit of Mother Teresa, the youth movement focused on works of mercy for the sick, the needy and the lonely around them.

In her address to the young people, Mother Teresa spoke sombrely of the Passion of Christ and of the stations of the cross by which he made his way to the place of crucifixion. As usual, she spoke without notes, making an unobtrusive sign of the cross with her thumb on her lips:

Today, in young people of the world, Jesus lives his Passion in the suffering, in the hungry, in the handicapped young people – in that child who eats a piece of bread crumb by crumb, because when that piece of bread is finished, there will be no more and hunger will come again.

That is a station of the cross.

Are you there with that child?

And those thousands who die not only for a piece of bread, but for a little bit of love, of recognition. That is a station of the cross.

Are you there?

. And young people, when they fall, as Jesus fell again and again for us, are we there as Simon Cyrene to pick them up, to pick up the cross?

The people in the parks, the alcoholics, the homeless, they are looking at you. Do not be those who look and do not see.

Look and see.

We can begin the stations of the cross step by step with joy. Jesus made himself the bread of life for us.

We have Jesus in the bread of life to give us the strength.

When the evening service was over, the young people, many deeply moved, came to thank her. They were grateful that she had talked of suffering and the cross, they explained, because of Eileen Potts. Mother Teresa showed surprise. She had never heard of Eileen Potts. The young people explained that it was Eileen Potts who had been the inspirer and leader of SIGN. She had herself arranged the evening for youth.

However Eileen had been unable to attend the youth Mass. Instead, she was in hospital. Eileen, at twenty years of age, had been struck down by leukaemia. Her friends were still shocked by the news, and asked Mother Teresa how she had known what to say to them that night. 'I don't know what made me talk like that,' said Mother Teresa to the grieving young people. 'It just came to me.'

Learning that Eileen was in a hospital near Philadelphia, Mother Teresa promised to visit her. On her return trip to

New York, Mother Teresa stopped at the Cherry Hill Hospital to sit with the young woman. The beautiful young girl was overwhelmed with joy to have a quiet time with Mother Teresa in her hospital room.

A photographer who had followed Mother Teresa's trip to the hospital took a photograph of the meeting which was to become a treasured memento for Eileen's parents and her friends. During a remission of the disease, Eileen returned to the University of Scranton to finish her studies, but death took her a few years later. She was an only child.

In her talk to the young people, Mother Teresa, in vivid examples, had pictured the suffering of the innocent, had described the need for responding to that suffering, and had pointed to the source of strength for that response. Through Mother Teresa's deep understanding of the power of innocent suffering, countless ordinary people, weighed down by loss and suffering, see their plight in a new and hopeful light. Like Shannon's mother, they realize that they are part of life's greatest drama.

Mother Teresa addressed herself to the suffering of the innocent in response to a query, 'How can a merciful God allow such suffering – children dying of hunger, people killed in earthquakes in Guatemala?' Mother Teresa spoke softly and meditatively:

> All that suffering – where would the world be without it? Innocent suffering is the same as the suffering of Jesus. He suffered for us, and all the innocent suffering is joined to his in the redemption. It is co-redemption. That is helping to save the world from worse things.

Mother Teresa was also invited to join a group of 300 theologians and leaders of various religious groups who had gathered to discuss the Eucharistic meal. When it was her turn to speak, Mother Teresa simply asked them to pray with her the prayer of Cardinal Newman: 'Lord help me to spread thy fragrance everywhere I go. Flood my soul with thy spirit and life.'

An earnest young woman, who was challenged by Mother Teresa's call to joyful service, queried her, 'But isn't it next to impossible to be a Christian in our society?' Mother Teresa replied:

> Yes. It is hard. And we cannot do it without help, without prayer. We have the body of Christ that gives us the strength we need. Jesus comes to us in the form of bread to show us his love for us, and he makes himself the hungry one so that we can feed him. He is always there, the hungry one, the homeless one, and the naked one.

In a similar vein, one Lutheran theologian remarked: 'The Eucharist loved is the Eucharist lived.'

Job and the Suffering Servant

❦

In Hebrew scriptures, suffering is linked to punishment for sin, both personal sin and the communal sin of the children of Israel. All sin is related to the original sin of disobedience of our first parents, the evil from which suffering and death ensue. Sin is followed by retribution, as presented in the calamities visited on Israel.

In the powerful drama of Job, however, another view of suffering shows itself. Job, the wealthy and pious man of Uz, is visited by a succession of evils. He is deprived of his children and stripped of all his possessions. He is left a derelict, scratching the sores that cover his body.

Job is resolute in maintaining his innocence. This is despite the insistence of his friends that he confess to the wrongdoing that he must have committed, evidenced by the disasters which had been visited on him. When his wife cries for Job to curse God and die, Job's response rings down the ages:

> Naked I came forth from my mother's womb,
> and naked I shall go back again.
> The Lord gave and the Lord has taken away;
> blessed be the name of the Lord.
>   *Job 1:21*

Job's trust was not shaken by all that he had endured, and his fidelity was rewarded by the return of his prosperity. Job's story lifts suffering away from any necessary tie to punishment for wrongdoing.

One has only to look at the teaching of Jesus to see that there is not always a direct cause-and-effect relationship between sin and suffering; to understand that the innocent sometimes *do* suffer. In dealing with the man born blind, Jesus corrected his disciples who wanted to place blame for the affliction on the man himself, or on his parents. The man's blindness, removed by the miracle of Jesus, occurred '. . . to let God's works show forth in him' (John 9:3).

In Isaiah 53 we see the prefiguring of the sufferings of Christ, of innocent suffering willingly borne:

> Yet it was our infirmities that he bore,
> our sufferings that he endured,
> While we thought of him as stricken,
> as one smitten by God and afflicted.
> But he was pierced for our offences,
> crushed for our sins;
> Upon him was the chastisement that makes us whole,
> by his stripes we were healed.
> We had all gone astray like sheep,

each following his own way;
But the Lord laid upon him
the guilt of us all.
Though he was harshly treated, he submitted
and opened not his mouth;
Like a lamb led to the slaughter
or a sheep before the shearers,
he was silent and opened not his mouth.
    Isaiah 53:4-7

Jesus, the long-desired Messiah, broke into history to incarnate the prophecy of the suffering servant.

Love Until It Hurts

❧

In *The Christian Meaning of Human Suffering* Pope John Paul II asserts: 'The world of human suffering calls for another world: . . . the world of human love.' This world of human love shines clearly in the life of Mother Teresa as she ministers to the needs of all those around her. Often I have watched her, palms together, fingers touching slightly, bowing in a gesture of respect to remind herself of the presence of Christ in each person she encounters. She and her helpers endeavour to ease the pain, loneliness, deprivation and confusion of the people around them, but the magnitude of such human suffering does not overwhelm the Sisters' human love, which is suffused with divine love.

By allowing God's Spirit to empower them, she told a group of lay-workers, they could go out to minister joyfully to those they met, following the example of Jesus himself:

As St Paul has said, '. . . the life I live now is not my own; Christ is living in me' (Galatians 2:20). Christ prays in me,

Christ works in me . . . Christ looks through my eyes, Christ speaks through my words, Christ works with my hands. Christ walks with my feet, Christ loves with my heart. As St Paul's prayer was, nothing will be able to separate us from the love of God, that comes to us in Christ Jesus, our Lord.

Romans 8:35-9

When Christ lives in us, we can love as Christ loves: a sacrificial love. Mother Teresa's simple way of driving it home is to say, 'Love until it hurts'.

Although she has seldom spoken of these experiences, Mother Teresa's life has been marked by times when she was called upon to do just that – to continue the work of love while accepting hurt and personal grief without complaint.

Joyful call, painful departure The first such experiences occurred when she was parted from her widowed mother, Drana Bojaxhiu. Mother Teresa was named Agnes Gonxha Bojaxhiu and she was only eighteen years old when she left a loving home in Skopje, in the former Yugoslavia. In those days, the decision of a young Catholic to be a missionary in a foreign land was a great sacrifice – it meant never seeing one's family again. Besides her mother, young Agnes left behind an older sister, Age, and an older brother, Lazar.

Her imagination had been fired by the stories sent back by priests from her area who had been stationed in Bengal, India. She wanted to join a mission there. Her time in Skopje, where Roman Catholics were a minority among a population of Orthodox Christians and Muslims, helped to prepare the young woman for her work in faraway Bengal, with its own religiously-divided society.

To India Accepted by the Sisters of Loreto (Institute of the

Blessed Virgin Mary), she lived briefly at their Mother House in Dublin. Then, with another young candidate she boarded a ship for the long voyage to India, in obedience to the clear call to serve God as a missionary. On 6 January 1929 (the Feast of the Epiphany) she arrived in Calcutta, a sprawling port city of the province of Bengal where wealth and culture flourished not far from utter destitution.

The Loreto Sisters from Ireland had been running schools for girls for nearly a century in the teeming metropolis. The city was a meeting place for great currents of thought, for poets and philosophers like Nobel Prize winner Rabindranath Tagore. At the same time it was a focal point for all the problems of Asia. As they opened schools for girls from more comfortable families, the Loreto Sisters also opened schools for the poor, and institutions for orphans.

The young nun from Skopje, now known as Sister Teresa, was so effective as a teaching Sister that she was named the headmistress of a school run by the Indian branch of Loreto, the Daughters of St Ann.

Independence With the Second World War, famine came to northeastern India. Rural people flocked from the reaches of Bengal to Calcutta's soup kitchens. Many perished: their bodies were burned in the crematory *ghats* next to the nearby Hooghly River.

The movement for Indian freedom from British rule had been building up during the years of the Second World War. Mohandas K. Gandhi, the Mahatma ('great soul'), had gathered a mighty following of *satyagrahis*, non-violent fighters for freedom. They were mostly Hindus, but many Muslims and members of the Christian minority participated as well. Gandhi had hoped for an undivided subcontinent, where the water and other resources could be shared. But Muslim leadership called for a separate Muslim state, and they won their case. When India became free of British rule on 15 August 1947, three states were formed: the primarily Hindu state of India, and the primarily Muslim states of East and West Pakistan.

Caught in the middle of the upheaval, displaced Muslim and Hindu families fled to their respective new homelands. Trains were crowded; oxcarts filled the roads; countless men, women and children died by the roadside. Since Bengal had nearly equal numbers of Hindus and Muslims, the travail was even more intense in the newly-partitioned region than elsewhere. In the capital city of Calcutta, communal violence between the Hindu and Muslim communities had often darkened the streets with blood. By far the worst riot in Calcutta's history erupted on 16 August 1946, the 'Day of Great Killing', during which at least 5,000 people died.

'Call within a call' About a month after that riot, on 10 September 1946, Sister Teresa experienced a second call, a 'call within a call', to work on the recently blood-spattered streets that now thronged with the homeless. God's voice in her spirit seemed clearly audible above the noises of the train compartment in which she was travelling to Darjeeling.

> It was on that train that I heard the call to give up all and follow him into the slum – to serve him in the poorest of the poor.

Years later Mother Teresa explained to her Sisters:

> When there is a call within a call, there is only one thing to do, to say 'yes' to Jesus. That's all. If we belong to him, he must be able to use us without consulting us . . . I had only to say a simple 'yes'.

But to leave the community of Loreto was a difficult wrench

of Sister Teresa's heart, equal to the parting from her own family. Replacing the voluminous floor-length habit with the rough sari of the poor, she walked out into the streets on sandalled feet.

Sister Teresa knew she belonged there, but she did not know to what work God would lead her. She went first to the school-less, near-naked children in shanties around a black sump-water pond called *Moti Jihl*, 'Pearl Lake'. She gathered the children around her and taught them the alphabet by drawing the letters in the dust with a stick.

She took her food with her, wrapped in paper. At midday, she knocked at the door of a convent to ask for water to take with her meal. She was given water, but was told to go to the back of the building. There she sat on the back stairs and ate her food like a street beggar. She was tempted to return to her dear community of Loreto, she recalls, but knew she had to persist in her new calling.

In her journal, she wrote:

> God wants me to be a lonely nun, laden with the poverty of the cross. Today I learned a good lesson. The poverty of the poor is so hard. When I was going and going till my legs and arms were paining, I was thinking how the poor have to suffer to get shelter.

The cool reception she received from many Calcuttans was not surprising. A lone European nun making her way to the alleyways of the poor in the garb of the poor aroused incredulity. Why would a gifted teacher frequent places where sewage ran in rivulets near the shanties? Even the missionary priests found it hard to understand. One of them, who later became a strong supporter, candidly admitted, 'We thought she was cracked.'

A family reunion The years went by. She was joined in her street work by some of her former students. Sister Teresa became Mother Teresa and her group of workers became the Missionaries of Charity. In time the rigid rules of missionary life began to change, and it would have been possible for Mother Teresa to visit her mother and sister had they not lived in Albania, which had become a closed country. (They had moved to Tirana after the Second World War.) When I accompanied Mother Teresa to Rome in 1960, after her first visit to the United States, she was reunited with her brother Lazar, who had married an Italian woman, and also met her only niece, Agi. On this visit Mother Teresa was able to request an official recognition from Rome of the Missionaries of Charity.

Drana Bojaxhiu wrote that her one wish in life was to see her daughter again. However, Mother Teresa's mother and sister were not permitted to join the rest of their family in Rome. The Albanian Government, sealed off from the rest of Europe, would issue no visas. Mother Teresa appealed to Albanian officials in Rome to allow her mother and sister to join her and her brother, who was ready to share his home with them, but the officials remained firm.

Mother Teresa suffered as she learned that her mother's health was failing. She, whose heart was open to the world and who helped all within her reach, was unable to help the one who had given her life. Mother Teresa's uncomplaining, silent grief over this deprivation allowed her to more deeply identify with the suffering of the innocent, especially those in exile around the world who are separated, often for ever, from their own loved ones. More years passed, a decade; but nothing could move the Albanian officials. Finally news came of her mother's death, and then that of her sister.

She had hoped against hope to enter the officially atheist country of Albania, home place of her ancestors, and would say, 'It will happen in God's time.' When at last Albania — along with the Soviet Union and Eastern Europe — threw open its doors to the outside world, Mother Teresa was finally a most welcome guest. Undoubtedly, she was the most famous person of Albanian origin in the world.

Her visit, however, was bittersweet. A photograph taken in a Tirana cemetery in 1990 shows Mother Teresa kneeling at the grave of her mother and sister. The long-sought reunion could only occur at their burial place. By that time, her brother Lazar had also already died. At eighty years old, she was the only one left of the original family of five. Poignantly, Mother Teresa observed:

> We will meet in heaven. When I go home to God, for death is nothing else than going home to God, the bond of love will be unbroken for all eternity.

On native soil Mother Teresa's personal grief was intensified by the knowledge of the deprivations of the Albanian people and of the persecution visited on believers in her native country. When she was permitted to re-enter Albania she witnessed abysmal spiritual as well as material poverty. During its isolation from the rest of Europe, Albanian authorities had persecuted all religions without mercy; during that time at least 160 Catholic priests had been killed. Many innocent citizens continued to suffer from the persecution.

Bringing in teams of Missionaries of Charity, Mother Teresa began to set up homes for orphans and abandoned children. One building, given to her by the authorities, had once been a mosque, she discovered. The Sisters cleaned it, made it habitable for the children and then turned it over to Muslim authorities, believing that God is the ultimate provider for the innocents of the world, whether here or in eternity.

5
Simplicity
The Joy of Material and Spiritual Poverty

❧

> Be compassionate, as your Father is compassionate. Do not
> judge, and you will not be judged. Do not condemn, and
> you will not be condemned. Pardon, and you shall be
> pardoned. Give, and it shall be given to you. Good measure
> pressed down, shaken together, running over, they will
> pour into the fold of your garment. For the measure you
> measure with will be measured back to you.
>
> *Luke 6:36-8*

In their first days in Harlem, the Missionaries of Charity
began their work slowly and simply by getting to know the
people and their needs. Mother Teresa recalls:

> When the Sisters came to Harlem, they began to visit the
> old people, the shut-ins who often lived alone. They would
> do the simple things, clean the rooms, wash the clothes.
>
> Once they came to a door and no one answered. The
> woman [who lived inside] had been dead for five days and
> no one knew – except for the odour in the hallway. So
> many people are known only by the number on their door.
>
> The worst disease today is not leprosy; it is being
> unwanted, being left out, being forgotten. The greatest
> scourge is to forget the next person, to be so suffocated
> with things that we have no time for the lonely Jesus – even
> a person in our own family who needs us.

Maybe if I had not picked up that one person dying on the street, I would not have picked up the thousands. We must think, '*ek*' [Bengali for 'one']. I think, *ek, ek*. One, one. That is the way to begin.

One of the difficulties with the English language is the confusion which can occur between some words, for example the word 'joy' with the word 'happiness'. Americans are aware that their Constitution contains the phrase 'the pursuit of happiness', and sometimes mistakenly assume that happiness always can be found, if it is pursued. Followers of Jesus realize, on the other hand, that happiness is a by-product, often unsought, of activities which may also have onerous aspects. A further confusion arises from the fact that happiness is often associated with pleasure. Certainly happiness and pleasure can be achieved, but they are short-lived – perhaps a moment, a day, a limited time. 'The joy of Christ risen', so central to Mother Teresa's teaching, is something that persists. This is the true joy that becomes a habit of the heart and persists through pain, suffering and the trials of life that are part of the human condition.

For most people, the very word 'poverty' suggests suffering: going without enjoyable comforts, pleasurable activities – the renunciation of the good things that society offers. Poverty, as lived in the vowed life and by many lay followers of Jesus, is rather the stripping of life to its essentials. As Mother Teresa warned her first recruits, 'You will have to renounce yourself. Your life will require constant self-denial.' Rather than suffering, this poverty brings with it a certain carefree joy, a dependence on God, a willingness to enjoy simple things. Such poverty, however, is not to be confused with destitution. Poverty, in this context, denotes having enough to meet one's basic needs.

The call to simplicity does indeed involve giving up the worldly things that distract us from our true calling, but it is a renunciation which does not despise the world and all it offers. Instead, it relinquishes even good things for a greater good. In the rule of the Missionaries of Charity, Mother Teresa writes:

> Let us not look for substitutes which restore to us the wealth we have given up. Christ, who emptied himself to work out our redemption, calls us: to listen to the voice of the poor, especially in our times. This, in turn, urges us to make reparation for the selfishness and greed of man, craving for earthly riches and power to the point of injustice to others.
>
> Our poverty should be true Gospel poverty: gentle, tender, glad and open-hearted, always ready to give an expression of love. *Poverty is love before it is renunciation.*

Poverty is so often seen solely as the lack of material things, of food, of clothing, of shelter. But it means more than that. It represents a more fundamental need that is often forgotten. Even in the poorest communities and the poorest countries, it is never enough to meet only the need for rice, for a garment, for some sort of shelter. Mother Teresa sees the larger reality:

> Today our poor of the world are looking up at you. Do you look back at them with compassion? Do you have compassion for the people who are hungry? They are hungry not only for bread and for rice, they are hungry to be recognized as human beings. They are hungry for you to know that they have their dignity, that they want to be treated as you are treated. They are hungry for love.

A daily prayer in the prayer book of the Missionaries of Charity comes from Pope Paul VI: 'Make us worthy, Lord, to

serve our fellow men [and women] throughout the world
who live and die in poverty and hunger. Give them through
our hands, this day their daily bread; and by our understanding love, give peace and joy.' This attitude of praying
to be worthy to serve God's poor shines through the work
of the Sisters.

In 1976, when she spoke to the Habitat Conference in
Vancouver, Canada, Mother Teresa began with this prayer.
As she spoke she noticed that a young woman with flying
fingers translated the words into sign language for the deaf
people in the audience. The hall was filled, but in the front
rows were special guests: long benches of the deaf and
dumb; of wheelchair-bound people with elephantine,
useless legs, or with necks held in metal braces. Moved by
the sight of these special guests, she started by declaring
her unity with them:

> We are all handicapped in one way or another. Sometimes
> it can be seen on the outside; sometimes it is on the inside.
> You and I come together not to plan any big thing, but to
> give until it hurts. The poor and the needy enrich us.

Mother Teresa did not leave the hall until she had shaken
the hand of each person in a wheelchair and of each mute
person on the long benches. A crush of participants was
waiting, each wanting a word with her or just to shake her
hand. But first she insisted on honouring the least in that
hall. Her prayer was to be worthy to serve them and to
bring them joy. That joy I saw in the glistening eyes of many
of the disabled.

A Double Poverty

❦

A double poverty is contained in the special witness of Mother Teresa and the Missionaries of Charity – the poverty of the giver, as well as the poverty of the receiver.

The Sisters live with utmost simplicity. When the order first started, each Sister owned two saris – one to wear and one to wash. In time, they could own three – one to wear, one to wash, and a third to mend. Their careful mending and reweaving of the rough cotton allows them to use one cheap sari for years. The Constitution of the Missionaries of Charity states:

> Desiring to share Christ's own poverty and that of the poor, we should be poor both in fact and in spirit – as individuals, as a community, and as a society. We shall have great simplicity of life and freedom from all unnecessary and artificial needs, retaining at the same time the spirit of total liberty in the use of created things when necessary.

Because the Sisters are often called upon to move from highly-developed societies to less-developed parts of the world, the call to poverty has a practical element as well: promoting unity of spirit among all the Missionaries of Charity and enabling them to move freely from one house to the next, wherever they are called to serve. In the documentary film *Mother Teresa* the Sisters in a newly-opened house in the United States are shown removing the serviceable rugs that kind volunteers had installed in their convent and throwing them out of the window. They knew that such luxurious floor covering would not be theirs in a house in another country or continent. Meanwhile, the Sisters politely explained to the donors that a more fitting use could be found for the carpeting. While this might

strike some as an extreme case of ingratitude, for the Sisters
it is a sign of solidarity. How could the Sisters in a house in
New York or in San Francisco enjoy soft rugs on the floors,
for example, when their Sisters in Papua New Guinea have
only hard cement?

Even when boiling August heat envelopes New York, the
Sisters have no electric fans to cool the convent quarters.
They would not have such fans in New Guinea, in Israel, in
Jordan, in Ethiopia, or in Haiti. Indeed, neither do the
Sisters have fans to counter the murderous heat of Calcutta.

The Sisters 'live lightly upon the earth', faithful to a
lifestyle that many might call ecologically sound. At the
same time, the voluntary poverty of the Sisters helps them
to identify with the involuntary poverty of the poor around
them.

Mother Teresa goes to great lengths – some people think
absurd lengths – to preserve this poverty. She relates:

> I remember when we first came to New York, and Cardinal
> Cooke wanted to give every Sister $500 every month. And I
> looked at him, I said, 'Cardinal, do you think God is going
> to be bankrupt in New York?' He looked at me. I believe he
> thought, 'Maybe she's a little bit off.' He has brought it up
> again, again, and again, and each time I answered the same
> way.

In Paris there was a similar experience. Mother Teresa
recounts:

> When our Sisters went to Paris to begin the work, the
> Church leaders explained about health insurance. They
> were going to have all the Sisters insured and they had the
> forms ready.
>
> I said, 'No, that is not for us.' Everybody was shocked
> and tried to make me change my mind. But I asked them,

'Do the poor that we work with have health insurance?'

That settled it. If we live with the poor, we must share their poverty and depend on the providence of Almighty God for his help. That is our faith.

Mother Teresa follows many holy people from the past, and numbers of vowed and lay Catholics today, in a rock-like dependence on the providence of God. She told a group of volunteers:

We do not accept any government grants. We do not accept Church maintenance. We have no salaries, receive nothing for the work that we do. So we fully depend on divine providence. We deal with thousands and thousands of people, and there never has been a day when we have to say to somebody, 'Sorry, we don't have.'

We cook for about 9,000 people every day in Calcutta. One day the Sister came to me and said, 'Mother, there's absolutely nothing. We don't have anything at all.' I couldn't answer her.

About nine o'clock in the morning a large truck full of bread came to the door. The schools were closed that day. They dropped thousands of loaves inside our walls, and the people had nice bread for two days. How he gives, how he brings things. That is how we are able to care for thousands upon thousands of lepers.

I was not surprised when I heard about the truckload of bread. I did feel gratitude that our Lord keeps showing his daily care for all his children, and especially for the poor. Occasionally God's providential kindness takes forms which intensify our gratitude and reduce our anxiety about our own resources.

On another occasion, Mother Teresa pointed out:

Our dependence on divine providence is a firm and lively

faith that God can and will help us. That he can is evident,
because he is almighty; that he will is certain because he
promised it in so many passages of Holy Scripture and
because he is infinitely faithful to all his promises.

Christ encourages us to have this confidence in whatever
we ask in prayer, to believe that we have received it
(Matthew 18:19). The apostle St Peter also commands us to
throw all cares upon the Lord, who provides for us (1 Peter
5:7). And why should God not care for us, since he sent us
his Son, and with him, all?

The generosity of the poor themselves is always a source of
delight for Mother Teresa. One of her favourite stories, and
thereby one of her frequently repeated examples, concerns
a family of poor Hindus. She loves to narrate:

> I had the most extraordinary experience with a Hindu
> family who had eight children. A gentleman came to our
> house and said, 'Mother Teresa, there is a family with eight
> children; they have not eaten for so long; do something.' So
> I took some rice and I went there immediately. And I saw
> the children – their eyes shining with hunger. I don't know
> if you have ever seen hunger. But I have seen it very often.
> And the mother took the rice, divided it, and she went out.
>
> When she came back, I asked her, 'Where did you go?
> What did you do?' She answered simply, 'They, the
> neighbours, are hungry also.' What struck me most was that
> she knew – and who are they? a Muslim family. I didn't
> bring more rice that evening because I wanted them to
> enjoy the joy of sharing.

Mother Teresa always follows this narration urging us to
enlarge our hearts with self-forgetting generosity and a
joyful trust in a loving providence.

Suffering in God's Love

❦

It was near Christmas and in one of the many slums (*bustees*) of Calcutta lived a cluster of leper families whose ramshackle huts huddle beside a pipal tree. To this desolate community the ambulance of the Missionaries of Charity came regularly, bringing a doctor-specialist and Sisters trained in anti-leprosy work. I went to distribute food, since supplying medicine without extra food would accomplish nothing. Mother Teresa later told us of talking with the lepers:

> I was talking to our lepers and telling them that the leprosy is a gift from God, that God can trust them so much that he gives them this terrible suffering. And one man, who was completely disfigured, started pulling at my sari. 'Repeat that,' he said. 'Repeat that this is God's love. Those who are suffering understand you when you talk like this, Mother Teresa.'

Wherever they go in the world, the Sisters carry out the guiding spirit of their Constitution:

> In fulfilment of our special mission in the Church, following the lowliness of Christ, we shall remain right on the ground, by living Christ's concern for the poorest and lowliest.

When they arrived in Lima, Peru, the Sisters sought out the lowliest inhabitants and gathered them into a large, empty convent. It was arranged Spanish-style, around a large square patio. The convent was known as *Hogar de la Paz*, the Home of Peace. When I visited the Home of Peace, the abandoned of every age and affliction were being cared for. Sister Pauline showed us the home and was especially happy that a practical vegetable garden was growing in the patio, alongside peach and lemon trees.

On one side, next to the kitchens and washrooms, were the children; on another side, sick and elderly women; and on a third side, destitute and homeless men. Standing on the fourth side of the rectangle was a large chapel which had once served the large community of Sisters as well as the surrounding district. The convent of the Missionaries of Charity, along with a second, much smaller chapel, occupied rooms on the second floor of the spacious building.

Mother Teresa walked about the dusty, unused larger chapel, surveying the cracks in the wall. It needed structural repairs before it could serve as a sanctuary for the Missionaries of Charity and for the crowded *barriada*. It could accommodate at least 400 people.

We talked with the residents, some very old, some nearly blind, some hardly able to move because of arthritis. Mother Teresa was particularly pleased that the doorkeeper for the Sisters' compound was named Jesús. One of the other residents bore the name of Messias. He was an articulate young man with classic features who had been a newspaperman and writer. A wasting disease had attacked his muscles so that he could only move about in a wheelchair. Messias told me that once he had had so many friends he could not number them, but when he could no longer earn his living and was confined to his room, he could not count on them. They did not want to see his affliction and left him alone. He still had hopes he would improve, and that some of his friends would rescue him.

He asked me for some books so that he could become proficient in English. I found an English grammar and Spanish-English dictionary in downtown Lima. When I presented them to Messias, his incapacitated neighbour, Theophane, told me that he, too, wanted to study English. Messias offered to help him. This was not merely a meaningless gesture of empty willingness. A letter from Sister Pauline informed me that Messias continued to practise so that he could speak English quite well, and he did help Theophane to learn the language, too. Both, she wrote, had caught the spirit of the *Hogar*.

The Sisters in Lima soon learned from a small group of priests that they were not wanted because their work was 'only a work of today', instead of a work that struck at the fundamental societal injustices that caused poverty. The critics felt that feeding the hungry and sheltering the helpless were a waste of time. But the Sisters persevered in their back-breaking work and were soon helped by residents of Lima, who came forward to volunteer with them. Mother Teresa's view was in keeping with the aim to 'remain right on the ground'. She explained:

> For us it's not a waste of time or life to spend that time just feeding the person today. The work of tomorrow? There are many people who can do that, who can remove the works of injustice and so on. But for us that person needs a shelter now. I think our part is fulfilled there. And by doing our part many people are getting concerned to do the second part – to improve and to help the people, to remove that poverty and that hunger and that nakedness.

The Community of the Poor

❧

Evidence is all around us that poverty brings suffering, especially to those who are helpless to change their lot. The living example of Mother Teresa and the Missionaries of Charity is a powerful one in dramatizing the fact that the involuntary poverty of the afflicted and deprived may be healed by those who move toward a measure of voluntary poverty. Their example speaks to millions in the world who possess more than enough to satisfy their needs.

Many already share their time, treasure and talents with generosity. Many could decide to share even more by giving, to use Mother Teresa's words, 'until it hurts'. The small suffering involved in such giving would lessen the vast suffering of a world in need.

Dependence on the providence of God, of course, must never be used as an excuse to escape from personal responsibility. Extreme interpretations of these principles of faith, for example, might tempt the head of a household to take a passive attitude toward supplying the needs of his family. Those people St Paul clearly cautions: 'If anyone does not provide for his own relatives, and especially members of his immediate family, he has denied the faith; he is worse than an unbeliever.' (1 Timothy 5:8)

God calls us to active and joyful service, wherever we may be, accomplishing the work he has given us today. To share the lot of the poorest ones is the particular daily task of the Missionaries of Charity. Mother Teresa's identification with the poor is instilled in the Sisters. May her spirit give us courage to follow her example.

My true community is the poor – their security is my security, their health is my health. My home is among the poor, and not only the poor, but the poorest of them: the people no one will go near because they are filthy and suffering from contagious diseases, full of germs and vermin-infested; the people who can't go to church because they can't go out naked; the people who can no longer eat because they haven't the strength; the people who lie down in the street, knowing they are going to die, while others look away and pass them by; the people who no longer cry because their tears have run dry!

The Lord wants me exactly where I am – he will provide the answers.

6

The Joy of Teaching by Example
Living in Love and Making Peace

❦

A man who listens to God's word but does not put it into practice is like a man who looks into a mirror at the face he was born with; he looks at himself, then goes off and promptly forgets what he looks like. There is, on the other hand, the man who peers into freedom's ideal law and abides by it. He is no forgetful listener, but one who carries out the law in practice. Blest will this man be in whatever he does.

James 1:23-5

Mother Teresa tells her Sisters:

Keep giving Jesus to your people, not by words, but by your example, by your being in love with Jesus, by radiating his holiness, and by spreading his fragrance of love, wherever you go. Just keep the joy of Jesus as your strength. Be happy and at peace. Accept whatever he gives you, and give him whatever he takes from you. True holiness consists in doing God's will with a big smile.

The life and work of Mother Teresa would have been instructive of the Gospel of Jesus even if she had never spoken a word in public or if no word of hers had appeared in print. Her example, along with that of the Missionaries of Charity, teaches us as powerfully as the spoken word.

The words of Mother Teresa become powerful simply

because they are so completely reflected by her actions. Deed and word are one, inextricably intertwined. The actions of the Sisters produce stunning and often unexpected effects on people. Mother Teresa relates:

> A Hindu gentleman stood, unnoticed, behind a young Sister who was washing a man just brought into the Home for the Dying. After a time, the man came to me and he said, 'I came into this home empty, full of bitterness and hatred, godless. I am going out full of God. I saw the living love of God through the hands of that Sister, the way she was touching and caring for that man.'
>
> He did not say another word and he left.

Face to Face with Sin

❧

The light of Christ shines most brilliantly in the places of greatest darkness. Some years after the end of the Second World War Mother Teresa and I visited the Dachau concentration camp near Munich, preserved as a memorial of hate and destruction. Over 2,500 Catholic priests, many of them Polish, were among the tens of thousands of human beings that are known to have perished in Dachau.

As Mother Teresa prayed on those bloodstained acres, her face clouded over with intense grief. At the end of a row of blockhouses was a round tower constructed of rough stones. Above the tower was a jagged crown of thorns, made of shining copper. It was the Chapel of the Agony of Christ, a reminder of all innocent suffering, dedicated to all who had died in the concentration camp. Mother Teresa said softly:

Colosseum. This stands for the Colosseum of our day. Then it was the pagans who threw innocent people to their death. It was not idolaters of those pagan gods who threw these lives away – and how many millions of them. We are getting worse, not better.

As we walked slowly out of Dachau she said, 'How could some human beings do these things to other human beings?' We were face to face with the mystery of sin, face to face with the senseless destruction of life. We saw what the human will is capable of when it exerts its freedom by turning from the law of God. We can choose to reject grace, becoming unspeakably cruel, destroying the children of God. In such actions, the sacredness of human life is negated. This time, it was expressed in the construction of death camps and the Holocaust of a people.

In Dachau, Mother Teresa saw that which was diametrically opposite to her life's mission. Devoted to the showing forth of the deepest affinity between the human and divine, she starts with her own relationship to Jesus:

> By blood and origin, I am all Albanian. My citizenship is Indian. As to my heart, I belong entirely to the heart of Jesus.

Jesus Living in Us

Mother Teresa's identity with Jesus gives her the clean heart necessary to see Jesus in those from whom the world turns away. It gives her the power to see each human being, even those rotting with disease, as repositories of the divine.

God's Spirit, freely communicated to the human soul

through grace, is most fully communicated through the gift of Jesus himself. Those who would emulate Mother Teresa's conviction of belonging entirely to Jesus might be moved to follow her in her openness to the grace of God. Belonging entirely to Jesus and living a life of grace is not simply for those committed to the vowed life: it should be the aim of all followers of Jesus. It provides a focus for daily life and for carrying out Jesus' command to 'Love as I have loved you'. This is the redemptive life that led Jesus to Calvary. In all likelihood, it may lead his followers to self-denial and hardship.

The willing acceptance of innocent suffering, as Mother Teresa points out, is co-redemptive: joined with that of Jesus, it relieves the weight of sin on a fallen world. The sufferings of all the just and innocent are joined in this great mystery. Can any suffering be meaningless or lost, even the sufferings of those who do not understand why it is visited upon them, but who, like Job, refuse to curse God? Mother Teresa points out:

> Today the Passion of Christ is being relived in the lives of those who suffer. Suffering is not a punishment. God does not punish.

The experiences of Mother Teresa and the Missionaries of Charity may illumine some facets of the great mystery of suffering, and may help us in our lowest moments. Mother Teresa's example has brought light, hope and joy to count-less people worldwide. Her life can encourage us in our daily struggles, helping us as we too console the inconsolable and feed the famished.

While Mother Teresa's example is a source of tremendous inspiration, it is also important to remember her limitations; she, too, is human, prone to human limitations. People sometimes comment, when called upon for a particularly generous gesture of love or forgiveness, 'I am no Mother Teresa'. In response, Patrick Jordan, editor of *Commonweal* magazine, once commented: 'While we may not be Mother Teresa, Mother Teresa is one of us, ennobling our condition, drawing our deepest aspirations into focus, and helping us to recognize God's active presence in the world.'

A frequent reminder from Mother Teresa is:

> What you do, I cannot do. What I do, you cannot do. But together, we can do something beautiful for God.

Living Out the Words

On 25 April 1983, Mother Teresa was one of the speakers at an inter-religious gathering in London on peace and the needs of humankind, along with the Dalai Lama and other world figures.

For many years, the Missionaries of Charity maintained shelters for the homeless in some of London's most dismal streets. Mother Teresa went with the Sisters and volunteers to see the plight of those who had no shelter at all. Many homeless men and women swathed themselves in quilts and blankets and lay like mummies on park benches. Others, after wrapping themselves as warmly as they could, spent the nights in coffin-like containers fashioned from cardboard boxes.

When it came time for Mother Teresa to address the gathering, she did not talk in abstractions of the sufferings in far-off Calcutta. She talked about the concrete example of what she had just experienced in London. She brought into the hall the very presence of human beings, not too many minutes away, whose best shelter might only be cardboard coffins. When Prime Minister Margaret Thatcher met with Mother Teresa, she was given a description of those who had been failed even by the night shelter programmes of a great city. With Mother Teresa, the deed precedes the word in pointing to human misery.

Thanksgiving
❦

Calcutta had been a crucible of violence between Hindus and Muslims at the time of the partition of the subcontinent in 1947. But by 1975 it was a city of comparative peace. This was the year of the Silver Jubilee of the Missionaries of Charity who had been founded as an order on 7 October 1950. In addition to operating the Home for the Dying, they were conducting schools, leper stations, and Mother and Child clinics in sixty centres. Mother Teresa and the Sisters intended to share their own deep joy at having been privileged for twenty-five years to serve the poorest of the poor in this city.

At Mother Teresa's invitation, the two major religious factions – the Hindus and Muslims – joined in thanksgiving with the Sisters. They were delighted when 5,000 Muslims met them in the great 'lung' of Calcutta – the green stretches of the *maidan* ('park') where Calcuttans can breathe fresh air – to make their gratitude known. It was during Ramadan (the month of fasting for Muslims) and, respectful of Muslim custom, the Sisters met at a distance from the sea of white-garbed men.

The birthday of the 'Father of our country', as Mother Teresa calls Mahatma Gandhi, was also remembered during that week of thanksgiving. On 2 October, the Leprosy Rehabilitation Centre was dedicated as the *Gandhiji Prem Nivas Centre*, The Gandhi Centre of Love. Because the

Missionary Brothers of Charity had grown in numbers, the Centre was turned over to their care.

The example of Gandhi meant much to Mother Teresa and to large numbers of Indian Christians. He had urged Christians to *live* by the Sermon on the Mount, rather than only to *talk* about it. Gandhi's movement of 'truth-force' depended on the persuasive power of innocent suffering to cause self-rule to replace colonial shackles. He described the movement as 'the argument of suffering'. Mother Teresa and Gandhi agreed that the eventual achievement of peace – personal, communal and national peace – would be 'the certain result of suffering voluntarily undergone'.

At the celebration, the Jewish community of Calcutta expressed their joy through the rabbi of the synagogue, who prayed:

Almighty God, it is with a heart full of joy that we have assembled here to express our great joy and render thanksgiving on the occasion of the Silver Jubilee of the Society of the Missionaries of Charity, for their humanitarian and selfless work, and through them for the poor of the world.

'This is the day that the Lord hath made, we will be glad and rejoice therein.' And now the day Mother Teresa has hoped for has come . . . . We, the Jews of Calcutta, join in thanksgiving unto the Lord and pray that the Heavenly Father in his mercy preserves Mother Teresa and her band of workers, guard and deliver them from all trouble and sorrow. Hasten the days when the children of men understand that they have one Father, that one God created us all. Then shall the light of universal justice flood the world, and the knowledge of God cover the earth, as the waters cover the sea. Amen.

A Fragile Peace

❧

The peace did not last. In 1992 the long-simmering rivalry between the Muslim and Hindu communities in Calcutta erupted in violence when a Muslim mosque, built upon the birthplace of the Hindu god Rama, was destroyed by a group of Hindus. Calcutta exploded in waves of looting, burning and murder – not unlike the chain of events in 1947 that induced Gandhi to fast until the violence between the two communities subsided. One Sister wrote from Calcutta:

> Thousands lost their lives. Only army trucks helped calm the riots. We had to walk with raised hands for several days.
> Mother Teresa, as usual, braved everything and went by ambulance to all the hot spots where people needed rice, oil and bulgur wheat. She was asked by many groups to come and pray with them for peace.

At the same time, violence was rending apart her birthplace, the former Yugoslavia. Her family had been part of the Albanian community in the city of Skopje. Mother Teresa asked her sisters to pray incessantly for peace in India and in the world.

She stopped her work and concentrated on a letter to the press – an appeal for peace, asking all opponents to 'bring the joy of loving through the joy of sharing', and reminding them 'not to use religion to divide us'. Mother Teresa's peace message has meaning – not only for India, but for countless places in the world where violence destroys peoples' lives and livelihoods, and where religion and ethnic division are used to inflame the passions of destruction.

> My Brothers and Sisters in India and all over the world, we are all God's children, and we have been created for greater

things: to love and to be loved. God loves each one of us with an everlasting love – we are precious to him. Therefore, nothing should separate us. Religion is a gift of God and is meant to help us to be one heart full of love. God is our Father, and we are all his children – we are all brothers and sisters. Let there be no distinctions of race or colour or creed.

Let us not use religion to divide us. In all the holy books, we see how God calls us to love. Whatever we do to each other – we do to him because he has said, 'Whatever you do to the least of my brothers you do it for me.'

Works of love are works of peace – to love we must know one another. Today, if we have no peace, it is because we have forgotten that we are all God's children. That man, that woman, that child is my brother, my sister. If everyone could see the image of God in his neighbour, do you think we would still have such destruction and suffering?

Religion is meant to be a work of love. Therefore, it should not divide us. It should not destroy peace and unity. Let us use religion to become one heart full of love in the heart of God. For this we need to pray that we may fulfil God's purpose for us: to love and to be loved.

My brothers and sisters, let us ask God to fill us with the peace that only he can give. Peace to men of good will – who want peace, and are ready to sacrifice themselves to do good, to perform works of peace and love.

So please, please, I beg you in the name of God, stop bringing violence, destruction and death to each other, and especially in the poor who are always the first victims.

Let us remember that the FRUIT OF RELIGION is to bring the JOY OF LOVING through the JOY OF SHARING.

God bless you,
Mother Teresa, MC

In July 1992, Mother Teresa's peacemaking efforts were recognized by a United Nations agency. The Peace Education Prize of UNESCO (the United Nations Education, Scientific and Cultural Organization) was awarded to her. The citation said: 'The prize crowns a life entirely consecrated to the promotion of peace and to combating injustice.' With the prize went an award of $60,000 toward the continuance of her work.

Nobel Recognition

❧

The UNESCO prize was not the first time that Mother Teresa's empathy for the poor had received public recognition. Her awareness of the suffering of the poor, and the love that could relieve that suffering, were also central to Mother Teresa's address upon receiving the 1979 Nobel Peace Prize.

Her white cotton sari shone under the spotlight as her slightly stooped figure stood on the stage of the Aula Magna of the University of Oslo. Before she began her address, she asked everyone in the hall to join her in the prayer of St Francis, the poor man of Assisi (copies had been distributed before the ceremony).

> Lord, make me an instrument of your peace;
> Where there is hatred, let me sow love;
> Where there is injury, pardon;
> Where there is despair, hope . . .

intoned over 800 voices. Among the lifted voices were those of a king, a crown prince and his princess – as well as academics, diplomats, politicians, members of the armed forces in full uniform, and a large press corps.

Oh Divine Master, grant that I might seek
Not so much to be consoled, as to console;
To be understood, as to understand;
Not so much to be loved, as to love another.

For it is in giving, that we receive;
It is in pardoning, that we are pardoned;
It is in dying, that we are born to eternal life.

Of all the holy people in history, it is to Francis of Assisi that
Mother Teresa is most often compared. His poverty, his
compassion, and his dependence on the providence of God
are hers. Her Franciscan gesture of refusing the customary
Nobel Award banquet so that the money saved could go to
the poor resulted in an additional gift of $6,000, to be added
to the Nobel Prize fund.

Undoubtedly, Mother Teresa's address was the simplest
of all those ever delivered at a Nobel Award ceremony:

The poor are wonderful people. One evening we went out
and picked up four people from the street. One of them
was in a most terrible condition. I told the Sisters: 'You take
care of the other three. I will take care of this one that looks
worse.' So I did for her all that my love can do. I put her in
bed, and there was such a beautiful smile on her face. She
took hold of my hand, as she said one word only, 'Thank
You', and she died.

I could not help but examine my conscience before her,
and I asked, 'What would I say if I was in her place?' And
my answer was very simple. I would have tried to draw a
little attention to myself. I would have said, 'I am hungry; I
am dying; I am cold; I am in pain,' or something. She gave
me much more – she gave me her grateful love. And she
died with a smile on her face.

Like the man whom we picked up from the drain, half-eaten with worms; we brought him to the Home. 'I have lived like an animal in the street, but I am going to die like an angel, loved and cared for.'

And it was so wonderful to see the greatness of a man who could speak like that, who could die like that, without blaming anybody, without cursing anybody, without comparing anything. Like an angel – that is the greatness of our people.

And that is why we believe what Jesus has said, 'I was hungry, I was naked, I was homeless, I was unwanted, unloved, uncared for, and you did it to me.'

Mother Teresa often spoke of the abortions occurring around the world and she did so again on this occasion. She reminded her hearers of the sacredness of the child in the womb with the simple New Testament story: When Mary, awaiting the birth of Jesus, visited Elizabeth, who was to become the mother of John the Baptist, the unborn child in Elizabeth's womb leapt for joy.

He recognized the Prince of Peace, he recognized that Christ had come to bring the Good News for you and for me. And as if that was not enough – it was not enough to become man – Jesus died on the cross to show that greater love.

He died for you and for me, and for that leper, and for that person dying of hunger, and for that person lying in the street, not only of Calcutta, but of Africa and New York and London and Oslo. And he insisted that we love one another as he loves each of us. And we read in the gospel very clearly: 'Love as I have loved you' (John 13:34). We too must give to each other, until it hurts.

It is not enough to say 'I love God but I do not love my neighbour.' St John says that you are a liar if you say you love God and you don't love your neighbour. *How can you*

love God whom you do not see, if you do not love your
neighbour whom you do see, whom you touch, with whom
you live? And so, this is very important for us to realize that
love, to be true, has to hurt.

This is something that you and I can do – it is a gift of
God to be able to share our love with others . . . . Let us
keep that joy of loving Jesus in our hearts, and share that
joy with all we come in touch with. That radiating joy is
real, for we have no reason not to be happy, because we
have Christ with us. Christ in our hearts, Christ in the poor
that we meet, Christ in the smile that we give, and the smile
that we receive.

Choose the Way of Peace

❦

In July 1991, Mother Teresa was invited by a Community of
Reconciliation to Corymeela ('Hill of Harmony' in Gaelic) in
Northern Ireland. The Peace People community was
founded in 1981 in Belfast as an attempt to heal the tragic
wounds between the two major religious communities.
Mairaed Corrigan and Betty Williams received the Nobel
Peace Prize for their efforts to make peace an attainable
goal there. The work continues in Northern Ireland as the
Community of Peace People.

Mother Teresa found herself in a landscape of a special
kind of suffering – a suffering caused by ancient enmities.
This was the same kind of suffering she knew and experienced in Calcutta, with its repeated riots and acts of
violence committed by Hindus, Muslims and even British
soldiers. The hatred and distrust in both countries seemed
to be self-perpetuating. It was as if a great infected wound,

caused by events which happened before living memory, festered and caused new grief each year.

Mother Teresa's talk was held in a large tent overlooking the sea, fifty miles north of Belfast. There Mother Teresa came into contact with people from both sides of the conflict in Northern Ireland. She found herself in the midst of people who were mourning the men, women and children who had been cut down in the years of sporadic violence. Some had family members in prison. She talked in Gospel terms of love and forgiveness.

After Mother Teresa's talk, Mairaed Corrigan noted the importance of aligning word and deed. She commented: 'Mother Teresa said nothing I had not heard before or read from the gospels, but she brings the whole thing to life. I think what makes Mother Teresa's words so effective is that she is living out her words in her life.'

Ciaran McKeown, who had framed the Declaration of the Peace People, was also at Mother Teresa's talk, and later wrote that he had come in thanksgiving to Mother Teresa 'for her unknown help to me in some of the darker moments of the Peace People experience'. He offered an example of how Mother Teresa's tirelessness in the face of daunting schedules could provide enormous inspiration. 'Many's the late and lonely night', wrote McKeown, 'when exhaustion threatened to induce hopelessness in the struggle to suggest non-violence for Northern Ireland. The thought of Mother Teresa's tireless exercise of love, in vastly more intimidating circumstances, provided energy and strength.'

Mother Teresa told the people, McKeown continued, to be mindful of the suffering of Mary at the crucifixion of her son, and how 'entitled to be bitter, Mary was'. A woman who could see her only son subjected to a cruel death, and not respond with bitterness, might move some hearts to set aside their centuries-old bitterness.

Mother Teresa has spoken out for peace wherever she saw it threatened. Her appeal, coming as a cry from the heart of peace, could apply to any countries that are on the brink of war.

Early in January 1991, Mother Teresa wrote to two faraway Heads of State, begging them not to inflict the suffering of war on human beings. President George Bush and President Saddam Hussein received her impassioned appeal just before the unleashing of the Gulf War. Mother Teresa wanted to bring home to the two men the need for compassion, for recognizing the preciousness of life, and the unity of humanity under the Creator. In her appeal to the two presidents, Mother Teresa begged 'for the innocent ones', the ones who would continue to suffer months and years after the weapons were stilled.

I come to you with tears in my eyes and God's love in my heart to plead to you for the poor – and those who will become poor if the war that we all dread and fear happens. I beg you with my whole heart to work for, to labour for God's peace, and to be reconciled with one another . . . .

You have the power and the strength to destroy God's presence and image, his men, his women and his children. Please listen to the will of God. God has created us to be loved by his love and not to be destroyed by our hatred.

In the short term there may be winners and losers in this war that we all dread, but that never can, and never will, justify the suffering, pain and loss of life which your weapons will cause.

I come to you in the name of God, the God that we all love and share, to beg for the innocent ones, our poor of the world, and those who will become poor because of war. They are the ones who will suffer most because they have no means of escape. I plead on bended knee for them. They will suffer and when they do, we will be the ones who are guilty for not having done all in our power to protect and love them.

I plead to you for those who will be left orphaned, widowed and left alone, because their parents, husbands, brothers and children have been killed. I beg you please to save them.

I plead for those who will be left with disability and disfigurement. They are God's children. I plead for those who will be left with no home, no food and no love. Please think of them as being your children.

Finally, I plead for those who will have the most precious thing that God can give us, life, taken away from them. I beg you to save our brothers and sisters, yours and ours, because they are given to us by God to love and to cherish. It is not for us to destroy what God has given to us. Please, please let your mind and your will become the mind and will of God.

You have the power to bring war into the world, or to build peace. *Please choose the way of peace.*

I appeal to you – to your love, your love of God and your fellow man. In the name of God and in the name of those you will make poor, do not destroy life and peace. Let the love and peace triumph, and let your names be remembered for the good you have done, the joy you have spread, and the love you have shared.

Mother Teresa's attempt to stave off the war failed. The people of Iraq, especially the children, suffered the brunt of the hostilities, and many died. The Iraqi government now had enormous health problems to solve. Lack of full food rations and medical supplies (both due to an embargo) hurt not the élite, but children and the poorest families. The Iraqis struggled to reconstruct a bomb-shattered water-purification plant and a partially destroyed sewage disposal plant.

When the bombing stopped, Mother Teresa went to Baghdad to relieve some of the suffering of child war victims. Behind the Church of St Raphael, a church of the Chaldeans, two teams of Sisters laboured to help disabled and orphaned children, the most vulnerable and threatened members of the Iraqi population. However, what the Sisters, along with voluntary and even United Nations relief agencies, were able to do for the people of Iraq seemed to be all but negated by the embargo which prevented Iraq from meeting its own needs.

Watching Mother Teresa's efforts in spite of everything, I was reminded of something she had said to a group of Franciscan friars years before: 'Let us keep the joy of loving Jesus in our hearts, and share this joy with all we meet and so become carriers of God's peace.'

7

Count It Pure Joy . . .
The Secret of Prayerful Perseverance

❧

> My brothers, count it pure joy when you are involved in
> every sort of trial. Realize that when your faith is tested this
> makes for endurance. Let endurance come to its perfection
> so that you may be fully mature and lacking in nothing.
>   *James 1:2-4*

With her gift for the concrete, Mother Teresa illustrated a
mysterious and transcendant concept, that of the co-
redemptive power of innocent suffering, in her reply to the
halting question of a woman totally disabled with cerebral
palsy. It was in the setting of a church meeting. The
woman's words were difficult to understand due to the
incessant twitches of her head and body: 'What . . . can . . .
people like me . . . do?' As spasms contorted the woman's
face, Mother Teresa replied simply:

> You can do the most. You are the one who lives with Jesus
> on the cross every day. You pray for the work, and help
> and give us the strength to *do* the work.

Her answer is meant for any of the house-bound, the para-
lysed, the wheelchair-bound, the helpless sufferers
throughout the world whose agony seems to be useless to
themselves, useless to society and useless to the world at
large.

Here grace enters in, the grace to accept the suffering and

to unite it with the 'Lamb of God who takes away the sin of the world'. Christ's death, while it seemed the greatest evil, is, in reality, the greatest good. Jesus on the cross is a co-sufferer with every suffering human being. In him, we see the suffering of God with, and in, his suffering people. In him, we see the risen King and the empty tomb beyond suffering. In the words of Mother Teresa:

> Never let anything so fill you with pain or sorrow, so as to make you forget the joy of Christ risen.

Though it may be supremely difficult, she asks us to see 'suffering as a gift'.

> Like all gifts, it depends on how we receive it. And that is why we need a pure heart to see the hand of God, to feel the hand of God, to recognize the gift of God in our suffering. He allows us to share in his suffering and to make up for the sins of the world.

Some suffering is relatively minor but besets us every day in the form of vexations. We become tired and lose our joy because of the accumulated problems we need to conquer. One day in 1976, I had filled a conversation with a litany of problems, some seemingly insoluble. Mother Teresa remarked, 'Everything is a *problem*, Eileen. Isn't there another word?' I had no synonym to offer. She suggested, 'Why not use the word *gift?*'

Our vocabulary changed. The first time I used the new terminology was on our return from the Habitat Conference in Canada. Mother Teresa was extremely anxious to have time with her Sisters in New York. I had just learned that our flight had to be broken en route with a four-hour delay in Toronto. As I was about to explain the 'problem', I paused . . . 'Mother, I have to tell you about a *gift*. We have to wait four hours here and you won't arrive at the convent until very late.' Mother Teresa responded with a rueful smile.

Perhaps the most insidious suffering, and one that is often locked into the most secret compartment of the heart, is the fear of dying. Mother Teresa, in the Home for the Dying, faces dying men and women every day of the year. Numbers of them are young people, cut off from living before they have tasted life's joys or achievements. She relates how so many of them, loved and cared for in their last hours, pass into eternity with a look of peace on their faces, and a word of thanks on their lips. 'These are our treasures,' she says, mindful of their gift to the world. 'They die', she keeps reminding us, 'without blaming anybody, without cursing anybody.'

Mother Teresa reflects the love of God in reaching out to the afflicted. She tells us that dying is simply going home to the source of all love, God. Jean Vanier, author of spiritual books and founder of a movement to care for the retarded and mentally afflicted, made a remark in the course of a 1971 joint interview with Mother Teresa. He said he hoped that Mother Teresa would be holding his hand when he was dying. Mother Teresa, by her consoling, loving hand in the Home for the Dying, only points to the hand of God – consoling, loving, ever-present. 'No one dies alone,' she seems to be reminding us. The Creator, source of all life, is close to all his children. As earthly life ebbs, we are simply going home to the source of all love, the Creator of us all.

But what is the right response to the suffering we have brought on ourselves? This applies to all, since no one is without sin. St Paul reminds us, 'Where sin increased, grace abounded all the more' (Romans 5:20 RSV). Forgiveness, like grace, is there for the asking – in the firmament, as it were – ready for all who call. As the poet Christopher Marlowe reminds us in the play *Dr Faustus*:

See, see where Christ's blood streams in the firmament!
One drop would save my soul – half a drop: ah my Christ!

No Slums in Heaven

❦

Heart problems have brought Mother Teresa close to the gates of heaven on more than one occasion. The first time was in June 1983 during a visit to Rome, when Mother Teresa fell out of bed and later complained of a pain in her side. Hospital tests revealed that she was suffering from heart failure. Cheerful as always, Mother Teresa related:

> The doctor joked with me, 'I cannot say that Mother Teresa has a bad heart.'
> They told me that if the fall had not made me come to the hospital, I would have had a heart attack. See the wonderful ways of God. St Peter must have said, 'Hold her back there. There are no slums in heaven.'

During her seven weeks of enforced rest in hospital, her many visitors included the King and Queen of Belgium. Messages came from around the world, including one from Jyoti Basu, the communist Chief Minister of West Bengal, telling her that the people were concerned about her.

Mother Teresa's daily regimen now included regular heart medication and she was warned not to climb stairs. However, she did not defer to her health, but responded with joy at new openings for the work. After leaving hospital, she flew to Warsaw and, within a year, opened a novitiate there for candidates for the Missionaries of Charity.

Eventually Mother Teresa's failing heart needed a pacemaker. In 1991, on a visit to the Sisters in Tijuana, Mexico, she collapsed again. Brought to San Diego, California, through the efforts of lay Co-Workers, she was cared for in Scripps Medical Center. For a time she lay between life and death. Again she rallied, and again resumed her travels, moving between India, Eastern Europe, Latin America, Africa and the United States. Then in August 1993, in Delhi, India, Mother Teresa's heart failed once more. Even the action of the pacemaker was not sufficient to stimulate heart action. Doctors at the All-India Institute of Medical Sciences issued guarded bulletins about her condition.

Her eighty-third birthday was approaching when a birthday gift came for which Mother Teresa and the Sisters had long been praying: to bring the work to China. Mother Teresa had long wished to take the Sisters into the vast expanse of the Peoples' Republic of China. Already many young women of Chinese origin were counted among the Missionaries of Charity and were members of the teams active in Hong Kong.

Missionaries of Charity bring tender mercy to those from whom the world turns away, especially the innocent. Each time selfless love overcomes self-concern; each time we transcend our own needs to meet the needs of another, the world of redemptive love comes into being. The 'not yet' of the reign of God breaks into existence in 'the already'. And into this reign, joy enters.

During a short visit to China in 1985 Mother Teresa had met with Deng Pufang, the head of the Chinese Federation for the Disabled. Mother Teresa had offered to provide help for China's disabled and impoverished citizens. Deng, the son of the Chinese leader Deng Xiaopeng, was himself disabled, wheelchair-bound as a result of injuries he received when thrown out of a window by the Red Guards in the Cultural Revolution of the 1960s. Yet he said no. In turning down Mother Teresa's offer of help for all the country's poor, Deng made it clear that China could meet its own needs.

Mother Teresa, who yearned to relieve the pain of China's disabled and other victims of China's communist regime, had to accept the verdict of 'not yet'. She recognized that God would allow the Missionaries of Charity to enter China in his time – just as he had allowed them to go into Albania in 1990. But it seemed that God's time came more quickly than anyone had expected. In time for her eighty-third birthday on 26 August 1993, and still in the All-India Institute after her collapse from heart failure, Mother Teresa received a visa to pay another visit to China.

Upon her return to Calcutta from the Institute, Mother Teresa's condition worsened and a painful operation for the unblocking of arteries was necessary. Mother Teresa told the Sisters that she had offered up the pain for China and the work of the Sisters there. She had been advised to rest for three months but instead she began to make plans to leave for China in October, less than three months later.

Time Breaks All Walls Asunder

❦

Just before she was to leave for Beijing, on 16 October 1993, a visitor from Germany presented Mother Teresa with a replica of the Berlin Peace Clock. The creator of the eight-foot-high Berlin Peace Clock, a famous jeweller by the name of Jens D. Lorenz, made the presentation in the court-yard of Shishu Bhavan, the Children's Home.

The original Berlin Peace Clock had been displayed for the first time on 9 November 1989. That evening, one of the most dramatic events of the century occurred: the Berlin

Wall was torn down. In his presentation, Lorenz explained that the inscription on the Peace Clock and its replicas was: Time Breaks All Walls Asunder. Four replicas had been made and three of them had been given to Ronald Reagan, Mikhail Gorbachev and Helmut Kohl. The first replica, however, had been reserved for Mother Teresa.

Present for the ceremony were representatives of Calcutta's many religious communities, including monks from the Ramakrishna Mission, Sikhs and various Christian denominations. The children of Shishu Bhavan, many rescued from the streets, drains and dustbins of the city, danced around the Peace Clock before it was installed in the chapel of the Mother House of the Sisters.

Jens Lorenz, in his talk, put into context the significance of Mother Teresa's contribution to humankind:

> The walls between rich and poor, the walls which set apart religiously or politically fanaticized minds have not been dismantled: disease-like they progress on their invasive course, destroying communities which had once lived in peace.
>
> Through the sheer force of her faith, Mother Teresa has been helping to overcome such walls for over sixty years. In her devoted caring for others, she has never paid any heed to race, creed, nationality or ideology, always speaking the language of God's love.
>
> Mother Teresa herself has had to overcome many walls, including those of the order, for the Missionaries of Charity work outside the convent walls, living and working in poverty among the poorest of the poor. They help where help is needed, bringing comfort to the sick and suffering, feeding the hungry, restoring strength to the frail and praying for those who mankind has no power to help.
>
> The active compassion shown by Mother Teresa and the

Missionaries of Charity reveals a path to deliverance from the web of hatred and violence which continues to convulse entire regions of the world. This living humanity demonstrates every day, every hour, every minute, that the hope for a world without walls, a world of peace, tolerance and brotherhood is not a vain hope – and this hope will grow every minute, every hour and every day that people, wherever they may be, follow in their own way the selfless example of the Missionaries of Charity.

Finally, 'Borne aloft on the wings of zeal', as a bishop remarked, Mother Teresa took off for China on 19 October 1993. On her return to Calcutta, Mother Teresa told of her trip in a Christmas 1993 letter to her Co-Workers. This Christmas letter also came to be Mother Teresa's farewell to the Co-Workers, particularly to those not working directly with the Missionaries of Charity. (See Appendix 1).

Thank God I am back home. Thank you for praying with such faith and love for my intentions. Your prayers must have helped me, for Jesus took great care of me all along. I am sure you are all anxious to know how God, in his loving providence, directed everything during our visit to China and Vietnam.

In China, we first went to Shanghai and met the Archbishop of Shanghai. The next day we went to Beijing to meet Mr Deng Pufang, the head of the organization for the care of the handicapped. He himself is in a wheelchair as a result of an accident. He received us very kindly and said he looked forward to the day China could have the Missionaries of Charity reaching out tender love and care to the poor in that beautiful country. While in China we were able to visit the Cathedral of Our Lady of Sheshan who is patroness of China. It was beautiful to see the love and devotion that the Chinese people have to Our Lady. Let us continue praying that Our Lady may take this foundation under her special protection and make it a reality soon.

I was also able to go to Vietnam where I met the Archbishop who is very anxious to have a community of our Sisters there. There are many beautiful young Vietnamese girls wanting to become Missionaries of Charity.

My prayer for you this Christmas is that you too may experience the joy that comes from seeing Jesus in all the distressing disguises in which he comes, through circumstances and people in your home, your neighbourhood, your parish, your city.

Regrettably, no additional invitations or visas were extended to Mother Teresa or the Missionaries of Charity after her visit, despite Deng Pufang's kind words. But Mother Teresa was patient as always, remembering what had happened in Albania, in Cuba, and in many other countries.

All-Surrounding Love

❦

Mother Teresa's view of innocent suffering is that of Martin Luther King, Jr, who called it 'unearned suffering'. She also joins Mahatma Gandhi, who, like King, taught that love for opponents is shown by accepting abuse rather than inflicting retaliatory pain. This is the path to an eventual change of heart for one's enemies. Like Mother Teresa, both leaders taught that love does not seek vengeance, but instead is willing to walk through the dark valley of trouble for the sake of peace and reconciliation.

In a world anguished by suffering, it is the active compassion, taught and lived by Mother Teresa, that is animating many to look beyond their immediate circumstances to meet the needs of others. The insistence on continuing the works of mercy in the midst of conflicts, rather than assenting to engage in war, brings a more fundamental peace to the world than the mere temporary cessation of hostility. Mother Teresa was overjoyed when her works of active compassion and works of mercy for the human community, expressed by the Missionaries of Charity, were recognized by the Nobel Award as being authentic works of peace.

Mother Teresa asks us as the followers of Jesus to cling to him as the centre of our lives, and to receive as providence the role he provides for us to play. She encourages each one of us to become a true and faithful branch on the vine, Jesus, by accepting him in our lives as it pleases him to come:

> as the Truth . . . to be told;
> as the Life . . . to be lived;
> as the Light . . . to be lighted;
> as the Love . . . to be loved;
> as the Way . . . to be walked;
> as the Joy . . . to be given;
> as the Peace . . . to be spread;
> as the Sacrifice . . . to be offered in our families, and with
> our close neighbours, as well as our faraway
> neighbours.

Appendix 1
Do the Small Things with Great Love:
The Co-Workers of Mother Teresa

❧

The History of the Co-Workers

❧

Mother Teresa had shown from the early days of her work with the poor a rare genius for inspiring others to take part in the work. The Co-Workers, as the lay family of the Missionaries of Charity, grew out of the desire of ordinary men and women to volunteer their time and talents to Mother Teresa.

It was the simplest of organizations. All officers were called 'links' – local, regional, national and international. There were no dues – Mother Teresa had to curb the enthusiasm of early Co-Workers by forbidding any collecting of funds. Meetings were held as needed. In the case of national meetings in countries such as Italy, France or the United States, they were timed so that Mother Teresa could be present. Co-Workers with greater means paid for the fare and expenses of those without means. One of the meetings of the Co-Workers of the United States was held in a Cistercian monastery in a desert-like expanse in Utah. At the meeting/retreat, Mother Teresa stressed, 'If we really love Jesus in the poor, then our first connection must be with him. Only after that can we really see him in the poor.' Communication was maintained through reports, often simply copied, shared locally, nationally and internationally.

The Co-Workers started in Calcutta, where Mrs Ann Blaikie, an English woman living there, began to help in feeding and changing the children in the Children's Home, cradling in her arms tiny infants close to death. Soon other volunteers joined in the work, putting themselves at the disposal of Mother Teresa and the Missionaries of Charity. Men also volunteered at the Home for the Dying. Some men, like Rama Coomaraswamy, would help by clipping the fingernails and toenails of the patients. (Rama was moved to study medicine by his experience, and later became a medical doctor and psychiatrist in the United States.)

The Co-Workers took on many roles and offered much helpful support. Frank Collins, who was in the American consular service, devoted his free time to transporting Mother Teresa and the Sisters to slum clinics and leprosy stations. Women who knew English volunteered to teach it to the young women entering the Missionaries of Charity from every part of India. (Mother Teresa had decided that in view of India's many languages and dialects, English would be the standard language of communication.)

Eventually, simple guidelines for the Co-Workers were formulated by Mother Teresa and Ann Blaikie. They were translated into numerous languages as the Co-Workers were planted in various countries. On 23 March 1969 a simple Constitution was blessed by Pope Paul VI, and Ann Blaikie became the first international link of the International Association of Co-Workers of Mother Teresa.

An International Effort

❧

While Catholics formed the core of the Association, people of many spiritual paths, moved by the example of Mother Teresa and the Missionaries of Charity, joined with the Co-Workers. They shared the vision of the work. A Co-Worker of Mother Teresa is one who sees the presence of God in every human being and chooses to fully share in the real service of the poor, using hands to serve and hearts to love.

In the United States, the work of the Co-Workers was begun by Dr Warren and Mrs Patricia Kump of Minneapolis. Along with local young doctors and their wives, they reached out to ill and troubled individuals, and to those in nursing homes. The Kumps also prepared and mailed the Co-Workers' International Newsletter which contained examples of Co-Worker action around the world and up-to-date information concerning the growth of the Missionaries of Charity. Here are some examples of the loving service which Co-Workers do around the world:

In Australia, aboriginal children are invited to leave the 'reserve' to have meals and spend holidays with local families. Birthday parties and Christmas festivities bridge the gap between Australia's first people and other Australians.

In Mexico City, Co-Workers found that if they presented themselves regularly at the airline companies, they would be given the meals unused in-flight. They give this food to the Missionaries of Charity who serve it to the men, women and children living at the edge of the city searching among the rubbish tips for saleable items. These people appreciate the change from their basic food rations.

In the United States, the Sisters who run five AIDS hospices (in New York, Baltimore, Washington, Atlanta and

San Francisco) needed men who would give one night or more a week to care for the patients. Co-Workers came forward in each city. In a Mid-Western town, a group of Co-Workers came to the aid of a young mother struggling with four small children. She and her husband could barely meet their basic needs and the young mother had almost reached the breaking point. In a practical offer of support, one of the Co-Workers would cook the evening meal each evening and prepare the children for bed.

In Zimbabwe, one Co-Worker, a poor woman, sold a sewing machine, part of her livelihood, so that two hungry families in her neighbourhood could lay in stocks of food.

In South Africa, teams of Co-Workers volunteer seven nights a week at a night shelter. The shelter, at Usindiso (The Saving Place), provides hot meals and a place to wash for over a hundred people.

In Indonesia, young Co-Workers decided to volunteer regularly at a state home for disabled children. A young woman wrote, 'I sit with a child whose head is very big. He can't leave his bed, but he looks for me. I learn to love this poor little Jesus.'

Co-Workers Disbanded

❧

On 30 August 1993 Mother Teresa sent a letter in her own hand to leaders of the Co-Workers of Mother Teresa around the world. Her message was that the Co-Workers of Mother Teresa was to be disbanded as an international association. Some of the recipients were surprised, while others understood the change. They realized that Mother Teresa herself was in a period of frail health when she wrote to them. She could no longer give the attention to the Co-Workers that she had previously been able to give for twenty-five years.

The word was received and shared throughout the network of Co-Workers that the organization was to be dismantled. Mother Teresa explained, however, that the Co-Workers would continue to exist in a decentralized form. Only those who worked directly with the Missionaries of Charity, with the Sisters and Brothers, would be called Co-Workers. Others, who had performed their works of mercy under the name of Mother Teresa, would now carry on in the same spirit but without the binding link of the name. This applied to thousands of groups, from Japan to Indonesia, from Zimbabwe to South Africa.

Many remembered that Mother Teresa had often said, 'Never forget you are Co-Workers of *Jesus* in this work.' Now, more than before, each voluntary group would need to find its strength in prayer and its inspiration in seeing the face of God in the poor.

The Final Guidelines

Mother Teresa's advice had been and will be repeated in towns and villages around the world: 'Do the small things with great love.'

Co-Workers in all walks of life will continue to recite the prayer inaugurated by Mother Teresa in St James's Church, Piccadilly, London. (She had been chosen by an ecumenical group as the person to unite large numbers of the human family.)

Lead me from death to life,
    from falsehood to truth.
Lead me from despair to hope,

from fear to trust.
Lead me from hate to love,
   from war to peace.
Let peace fill our hearts, our world,
   our universe.
Peace. Peace. Peace.

The fullness of compassion Mother Teresa finds in Jesus; and through Jesus, the compassion of God. Others will continue to join her in doing the works of peace and love in accordance with their own vision.

The final guidelines of the Co-Workers began with a favourite reminder of Mother Teresa's:

> Love to pray – feel often during the day the need for prayer and take the trouble to pray. Prayer enlarges the heart until it is capable of containing God's gift of himself. Ask and seek, and your heart will grow big enough to receive him and keep him as your own.
>
> *God bless you,*
> *Mother Teresa, MC*

Appendix 2
National Prayer Breakfast
Washington, DC

❦

On 3 February 1994 the Annual National Prayer Breakfast was held at the Hilton Hotel in Washington, DC. Over 4,000 people filled the hall to hear Mother Teresa. She was flanked by President and Mrs Clinton, Vice-President and Mrs Gore, and the leaders of Congress. In the audience were many congressional members and their families.

On this occasion, Mother Teresa departed from her custom by reading from a prepared text. Even in her Nobel Peace Prize acceptance speech, Mother Teresa had had no prepared text. I had watched her in Oslo as she followed her custom of making an almost imperceptible sign of the cross on her lips with her thumb. Then she began to speak without referring to a single note. In Washington, the newspapers reported rapt silence in the hall as Mother Teresa spoke and an acclamation as she finished. What follows are excerpts from that speech:

> On the last day, Jesus will say to those on his right hand, 'Come, enter the kingdom. For I was hungry and you gave me food, I was thirsty and you gave me drink, I was sick and you visited me.' Then Jesus will turn to those on his left hand and say, 'Depart from me because I was hungry and you did not feed me, I was thirsty and you did not give me to drink, I was sick and you did not visit me.' These will ask him, 'When did we see you hungry, or thirsty or sick and

did not come to your help?' And Jesus will answer them, 'Whatever you neglected to do unto one of the least of these, you neglected to do unto me!'

As we have gathered here to pray together, I think it will be beautiful if we begin with a prayer that expresses very well what Jesus wants us to do for the least. St Francis of Assisi understood very well these words of Jesus and his life is very well expressed by a prayer. And this prayer, which we say every day after Holy Communion, always surprises me very much, because it is very fitting for each one of us.

I always wonder whether 800 years ago, when St Francis lived, they had the same difficulties that we have today. I think that some of you already have this prayer of peace – so we will pray it together . . . .

Let us thank God for the opportunity he has given us today to have come here to pray together. We have come here especially to pray for peace, joy and love. We are reminded that Jesus came to bring the good news to the poor. He had told us what is that good news when he said, 'Peace I leave with you; my peace I give unto you' (John 14:27). He came not to give the peace of the world which is only that we don't bother each other. He came to give the peace of heart which comes from loving – from doing good to others.

God loved the world so much that he gave his Son – it was a giving. God gave his Son to the Virgin Mary, and what did she do with him? As soon as Jesus came into Mary's life, immediately she went in haste to give that good news. And as she came into the house of her cousin, Elizabeth, Scripture tells us that the unborn child – the child in the womb of Elizabeth – leapt with joy. While still in the womb of Mary – Jesus brought peace to John the Baptist, who leapt for joy in the womb of Elizabeth.

And as if that were not enough, as if it were not enough

that God the Son should become one of us and bring peace and joy while still in the womb of Mary, Jesus also died on the cross to show that greater love. He died for you and for me, and for that leper and for that man dying of hunger and that naked person lying in the street, not only of Calcutta, but of Africa, and everywhere.

Our Sisters serve those poor people in 105 countries throughout the world. Jesus insisted that we love one another as he loves each one of us. Jesus gave his life to love us and he tells us that we also have to give whatever it takes to do good to one another. And in the Gospel Jesus says very clearly, 'Love as I have loved you.'

Jesus died on the cross because that is what it took for him to do good to us – to save us from our selfishness in sin. He gave up everything to do the Father's will – to show us that we too must be willing to give up everything to do God's will – to love one another as he loves each of us. If we are not willing to give whatever it takes to do good to one another, sin is still in us. That is why we too must give to each other until it hurts.

It is not enough for us to say 'I love God', but I also have to love my neighbour. St John says that you are a liar if you say you love God and you don't love your neighbour. How can you love God whom you do not see, if you do not love your neighbour whom you see, whom you touch, with whom you live?

And so it is very important for us to realize that love, to be true, has to hurt. I must be willing to give whatever it takes not to harm other people and, in fact, to do good to them. This requires that I be willing to give until it hurts. Otherwise, there is no true love in me and I bring injustice, not peace, to those around me.

It hurt Jesus to love us. We have been created in his image for greater things, to love and to be loved. We must put on Christ, as Scripture tells us. And so, we have been created to love as he loves us. Jesus makes himself the hungry one, the naked one, the homeless one, the unwanted one, and he says, 'You did it to me.'

On the last day he will say to those on his right, 'Whatever you did to the least of these, you did to me.' And he will also say to those on his left, 'Whatever you neglected to do for the least of these, you neglected to do it for me.'

When he was dying on the cross, Jesus said, 'I thirst.' Jesus is thirsting for our love, and this is the thirst of everyone, poor and rich alike. We all thirst for the love of others, that they go out of their way to avoid harming us and to do good to us. This is the meaning of true love, to give until it hurts.

I can never forget the experience I had in visiting a home where they kept all these old parents of sons and daughters who had just put them into an institution and forgotten them – maybe. I saw that in that home these old people had everything – good food, a comfortable place, television, everything, but everyone was looking toward the door. And I did not see a single one with a smile on their face. I turned to Sister and I asked, 'Why do these people who have every comfort here, why are they all looking toward the door? Why are they not smiling?' I am so used to seeing the smiles on our people, even the dying ones smile.

And Sister said, 'This is the way it is nearly every day. They are expecting, they are hoping that a son or daughter will come to visit them. They are hurt because they are forgotten.' And see, this neglect to love brings spiritual poverty. Maybe in our own family we have somebody who is feeling lonely, who is feeling sick, who is feeling worried. Are we there? Are we willing to give until it hurts in order to be with our families, or do we put our own interests first?

These are the questions we must ask ourselves, especially as we begin this Year of the Family. We must remember that love begins at home and we must also remember that 'the future of humanity passes through the family'.

I was surprised in the West to see so many young boys and girls given to drugs. And I tried to find out why. Why is it like that, when those in the West have so many more things than those in the East? And the answer was: 'Because there is no one in the family to receive them.' Our children depend on us for everything – their health, their nutrition, their security, their coming to know and love God. For all of this, they look to us with trust, hope and expectation. But often father and mother are so busy they have no time for their children, or perhaps they are not even married or have given up on their marriage. So the children go to the streets and get involved in drugs or other things. We are talking of love of the child, which is where love and peace must begin. These are the things that break peace.

But I feel that the greatest destroyer of peace today is abortion, because it is a war against the child, a direct killing of the innocent child, murder by the mother herself. And if we accept that a mother can kill even her own child, how can we tell other people not to kill one another? How do we persuade a woman not to have an abortion? As always, we must persuade her with love, and we remind ourselves that love means to be willing to give until it hurts. Jesus gave even his life to love us.

So, the mother who is thinking of abortion, should be helped to love; that is, to give until it hurts her plans, or her free time; to respect the life of her child. The father of that child, whoever he is, must also give until it hurts. By abortion, the mother does not learn to love, but kills even her own child to solve her problems. And, by abortion, the father is told that he does not have to take any responsibility at all for the child he has brought into the world. That father is likely to put other women into the same trouble. So abortion just leads to more abortion. Any country that accepts abortion is not teaching its people to love, but to use any violence to get what they want. This is why the greatest destroyer of love and peace is abortion.

Many people are very, very concerned with the children of India, with the children of Africa where quite a few die of hunger, and so on. Many people are also concerned about all the violence in this great country of the United States. These concerns are very good. But often these same people are not concerned with the millions who are being killed by the deliberate decision of their own mothers. And this is what is the greatest destroyer of peace today – abortion, which brings people to such blindness.

And for this I appeal in India and I appeal everywhere: 'Let us bring the child back.' The child is God's gift to the family. Each child is created in the special image and likeness of God for greater things – to love and to be loved. In this Year of the Family we must bring the child back to the centre of our care and concern. This is the only way that our world can survive because our children are the only hope for the future. As older people are called to God, only their children can take their places.

But what does God say to us? He says, 'Even if a mother could forget her child, I will not forget you. I have carved you in the palm of my hand.' We are carved in the palm of his hand; that unborn child has been carved in the hand of God from conception and is called by God to love and to be loved, not only now in this life, but for ever. God can never forget us.

I will tell you something beautiful. We are fighting abortion by adoption – by care of the mother and adoption for her baby. We have saved thousands of lives. We have sent word to the clinics, to the hospitals and police stations: 'Please don't destroy the child; we will take the child.' So we always have someone tell the mothers in trouble: 'Come, we will take care of you, we will get a home for your child.' And we have a tremendous demand from couples who cannot have a child – but I never give a child to a couple who have done something not to have a child. Jesus said, 'Anyone who receives a child in my name, receives me.' By adopting a child, these couples receive Jesus, but by aborting a child, a couple refuses to receive Jesus.

Please don't kill the child. I want the child. Please give me the child. I am willing to accept any child who would be aborted and to give that child to a married couple who will love the child and be loved by the child. From our Children's Home in Calcutta alone, we have saved over 3,000 children from abortion. These children have brought such love and joy to their adopting parents and have grown up so full of love and joy.

I know that couples have to plan their family, and for that there is natural family planning. The way to plan the family is natural family planning, not contraception. In destroying the power of giving life, through contraception, a husband or wife is doing something to self. This turns the attention to self and so destroys the gift of love in him or her. In loving, the husband and wife must turn the attention to each other as happens in natural family planning, and not to self, as happens in contraception. Once that living love is destroyed by contraception, abortion follows very easily.

I also know that there are great problems in the world, that many spouses do not love each other enough to practise natural family planning. We cannot solve all the problems in the world, but let us never bring in the worst problem of all, and that is to destroy love. And this is what happens when we tell people to practise contraception and abortion.

The poor have very great people. They can teach us so many beautiful things. Once one of them came to thank us for teaching her natural family planning and said, 'You people who have practised chastity, you are the best people to teach us natural family planning because it is nothing more than self-control out of love for each other.' And what this poor person said is very true. These poor people maybe having nothing to eat, maybe they have not a home to live in, but they can still be great people when they are spiritually rich.

When I pick up a person from the street, hungry, I give him a plate of rice, a piece of bread. But a person who is shut out, who feels unwanted, unloved, terrified, the person who has been thrown out of society – that spiritual poverty is much harder to overcome. And abortion, which often follows from contraception, brings a people to be spiritually poor, and that is the worst poverty and the most difficult to overcome . . . .

We are not social workers. We may be doing social work in the eyes of some people, but we must be contemplatives in the heart of the world. For we must bring that presence of God into your family, for the family that prays together, stays together. There is so much hatred, so much misery, and we with our prayer, with our sacrifice, are beginning at home. Love begins at home, and it is not how much we do, but how much love we put into what we do.

If we are contemplatives in the heart of the world with all its problems, these problems can never discourage us. We must always remember what God tells us in Scripture: 'Even if a mother could forget the child in her womb' – something impossible, but even if she could forget – 'I will never forget you.' . . .

God will never forget us and there is something you and I can always do. We can keep the joy of loving Jesus in our hearts, and share that joy with all we come in contact with. Let us make that one point – that no child will be unwanted, unloved, uncared for, or killed and thrown away. And give until it hurts – with a smile . . . .

One of the most demanding things for me is travelling everywhere – and with publicity. I have said to Jesus that if I don't go to heaven for anything else, I will be going to heaven for all the travelling with all the publicity, because it has purified me and sacrificed me and made me really ready for heaven.

If we remember that God loves us, and that we can love others as he loves us, then America can become a sign of peace for the world. From here, a sign of care for the weakest of the weak – the unborn child – must go out to the world. If you become a burning light of justice and peace in the world, then really you will be true to what the founders of this country stood for. God bless you!

Why would thousands of people turn out to be in the presence of a small, bent woman of eighty-three whom they could see behind the podium only by craning their necks? While many present that morning did not agree with her view on the protection of the unborn child, they came for something else – to see a person who had 'put on Christ', a person who in the twentieth century lived as Christ lived. President Clinton did not respond directly to Mother Teresa's statements on abortion, but he thanked her for 'her life of commitment', a commitment, he stated, that she had 'truly lived'.

When I met with Mother Teresa a few days later in the Harlem house of the Missionaries of Charity, she handed me the four-page copy of her talk. 'Wasn't this the first time you ever read a talk?' She agreed.

Mother Teresa recounted that after the Prayer Breakfast, President and Mrs Clinton had talked with her. She told them of the work in Calcutta, of the Shishu Bhavan where rescued children are cared for. 'Then I asked Mrs Clinton', said Mother Teresa, 'if we could have a house for children in Washington. I would be ready to send our Sisters to take care of it. Mrs Clinton said nothing for a while. She was thinking about it. Then she said, "Yes, I will help you to get a house." '

Mother Teresa talked of other plans. She hoped to open two houses in Vietnam: one in Hanoi, and the other in 'that other city', referring to the city of Ho Chi Minh. 'I still have hope for China,' she said.

Many people were grateful for her defence of life, including not only her objection to abortion, but to the killing of war and capital punishment as well. 'Not long ago,' she told me, 'a judge in the United States telephoned me in Calcutta. He asked my advice about a man who could be sentenced to death. All I said was, "Do what Jesus would do in your place." '

We talked about personal suffering: 'When someone does something that hurts you, let it pass through.' She pointed with her index finger to her left ear, and then to her right ear, as though the hurt were leaving, not remaining. 'Never let it stay here,' she said, placing her hand over her heart. 'When you do that, you can go on happily. You do not lose joy.' She continued:

> The important thing, is not to waste suffering. Join it to the suffering of Christ; offer it up with his suffering. Don't waste suffering.

Mother Teresa wants all people to see innocent suffering as part of the greatest drama of the world, the redemption of the human family.

THE PILGRIM'S PROGRESS

John Bunyan

Written in prison, where Bunyan had been sent for unauthorized preaching, and first published in 1678, this classic story has been described as the most popular work of Christian spirituality written in English, and as the first English novel. It describes the road to the Celestial City, by way of Doubting Castle, the Delectable Mountains, Vanity Fair and other places whose names have entered the very fabric of the language.

Fascinating as literature, entertaining as story, profound as spiritual teaching for the soul's journey, *The Pilgrim's Progress* is 'a masterpiece which generation after generation of ordinary men and women have taken to their hearts' (Hugh Ross Williamson).

Fount Classics
BIOGRAPHY

JOHN BUNYAN
The Christian
Gordon Wakefield

John Bunyan, born in 1628 son of a Bedford tinker, and
teenage soldier in the army of Robert Cromwell, fell into
a kind of religious madness and emerged from this a soldier
in the army of Christ: a fiery preacher in the radical
Puritan tradition. His fervour brought him into conflict
with the Restoration government, and he spent much time
in prison. It was there he wrote his famous masterpiece,
The Pilgrim's Progress. By the time of his death he had
written some sixty works.

This outstanding biography takes Bunyan seriously as a
spiritual guide, and sets his life in the context of the history
of English Christianity, as well as the political conflicts of
his time.

Gordon Wakefield was Principal of the Queen's College
Birmingham from 1979 until his retirement in 1987. He is
a Methodist minister and director of the Alister Hardy
Centre for Research into Religious Experience. He edited
A Dictionary of Christian Spirituality (SCM) and, in 1986,
was the first Methodist minister to be awarded the
Lambeth doctorate of divinity. He lives in Lichfield

'Wakefield's excellent book helps us to understand why
Bunyan's influence continues down the centuries and
across the continents   *Baptist Times*

'The chief merit of this impressive theological life is to
bring back a Bunyan with a vibrant word for now, one
that leaps all denominational frontiers'
Methodist Recorder

Fount Classics

AUTOBIOGRAPHY OF A SAINT
St Thérèse of Lisieux
Translated by Ronald Knox

St Thérèse of Lisieux, known as the 'Little Flower', who
died in 1897 virtually unknown outside her convent, is
now recognized as the most popular and influential saint of
our times. She was canonized in 1925, and successive
Popes have recommended her as an authoritative spiritual
guide for the twentieth century and beyond.

The immense popularity of Térèse is largely based upon
this book. It is her own personal testimony. Written at odd
moments in school exercise books and on scraps of paper,
it gives a vivid human account of the life of a saint from
the inside; intimate, spontaneous and sparkling throughout
with a delightful humour.

Ronald Knox was a witty and brilliant Anglican priest and
scholar who became one of this century's most famous
converts to Roman Catholicism, and went on in the 1940s
to make one of the greatest modern translations of the
Bible.

Fount Classics
BIOGRAPHY

THÉRÈSE OF LISIEUX

Michael Hollings

The most influential and most popular saint of modern
times, Térèse Martin died virtually unknown outside her
Carmelite convent in 1897, at the age of 24. After her
death came the storm of glory, the miracles and the
acclaim that swept her statue into every church and her
spiritual teaching into the mouths of Popes.
Thérèse's 'little way' of prayer was a message for humanity
of our time, and the publication of her own writings made
it known around the world. This vivid biography brings
the reader into the closest contact with the life and world
of Thérèse, often in her own words, and serves as an ideal
introduction to this 'little' mystic who inspires millions of
Christians.

Michael Hollings is Roman Catholic parish priest of St
Mary of the Angels, Moorhouse Road, Bayswater.

'. . . a gem of brief and yet deep biography . . . an account
which is sensitive and totally dispels any preconceived
notion of sentimentality in connection with 'the Little
Flower'. Father Hollings comments with great
understanding on her writings and special contribution to
spirituality . . . It is by far the best book I have ever seen
on this extraordinary woman' *Methodist Recorder*

Fount Classics

BIOGRAPHY

IGNATIUS LOYOLA

Philip Caraman

St Ignatius, founder of the Jesuits or Society of Jesus, was
born in 1491, the year before the discovery of the New
World by Columbus. He grew up in a golden age of the
Spanish court, himself a courtier, a knight, a gambler and a
ladies' man.

Philip Caraman is a member of the Society of Jesus and a
historian of world renown. His previous books include *The
Lost Paradise*, the story of the Jesuit Reductions in Paraguay
and the subject of the film *The Mission*, and the
international bestseller *John Gerard*.

'A brilliant and beautiful achievement'
ELIZABETH LONGFORD

'A vivid and veracious biography which all can enjoy for
its human and historical interest' A. L. ROWSE

Fount Classics
SPIRITUAL DIRECTION

FINDING GOD IN ALL THINGS
The Way of St Ignatius
Margaret Hebblethwaite

St Ignatius of Loyola, the sixteenth-century founder of the
Jesuits, left behind him a living tradition of prayer in his
Spiritual Exercises. Over the centuries these have been
enormously influential; today there is more interest than
ever in Ignatian spirituality, among ordinary people as well
as religious professionals, and across all the Christian
denominations.

In this book Margaret Hebblethwaite interprets the ideas of
Ignatius for the present day. She combines sound practical
advice on how to set about praying with an understanding
of the deep mystery and beauty of prayer; prayer which
can lead us, not to leave the world behind, but to make
full use of all our God-given opportunities so that we too
can learn to find God in all things.

Margaret Hebblethwaite was born in 1951, studied at
Oxford and at the Gregorian University in Rome. She is a
founder member and former committee member of the
Catholic Theological Association of Great Britain. Her
books include *Motherhood and God* and the recently
published *Basic is Beautiful*. She is now assistant editor of
Catholic weekly *The Tablet*.